W9-DET-592

STUDENT BOOK 2

JACK C. RICHARDS DAVID BYCINA SUE BRIOUX ALDCORN

NEW PERSON TO PERSON

COMMUNICATIVE SPEAKING AND LISTENING SKILLS

OXFORD UNIVERSITY PRESS

OXFORD
UNIVERSITY PRESS

198 Madison Avenue
New York, NY 10016 USA

Great Clarendon Street
Oxford OX2 6DP England

Oxford New York

Auckland Cape Town Dar es Salaam Hong Kong Karachi
Kuala Lumpur Madrid Melbourne Mexico City Nairobi
New Delhi Shanghai Taipei Toronto
With offices in

Argentina Austria Brazil Chile Czech Republic France Greece
Guatemala Hungary Italy Japan Poland Portugal Singapore
South Korea Switzerland Thailand Turkey Ukraine Vietnam

OXFORD is a trademark of Oxford University Press.

Library of Congress Cataloging-in-Publication Data
(Revised for vol. 2)

Richards, Jack. C.
    New person to person student book.

    1. English language—Textbooks for foreign speakers.
2. English language—Spoken English—Problems,
exercises, etc. 3. Listening—Problems, exercises, etc.
I. Bycina, David. II. Aldcorn, Sue Brioux. III. Title.
IV. Title: New person to person.

PE1122.R49   1995   428.2′4   94-17962
ISBN-13: 978 0 19 434678 8 (v.1)
ISBN-10: 0 19 434678 1
ISBN-13: 978 0 19 434681 8 (v.2)
ISBN-10: 0 19 434681 1

Copyright © 1995 Oxford University Press

No unauthorized photocopying.

All rights reserved. No part of this publication
may be reproduced, stored in a retrieval
system, or transmitted, in any form or by any
means, electronic, mechanical, photocopying,
recording, or otherwise, without the prior written
permission of Oxford University Press.

This book is sold subject to the condition that
it shall not, by way of trade or otherwise,
be lent, resold, hired out, or otherwise
circulated without the publisher's prior
consent in any form of binding or cover other
than that in which it is published and without
a similar condition including this condition
being imposed on the subsequent purchaser.

Editorial Managers: Chris Foley and Shelagh Speers
Editors: Kathy Sands Boehmer and Paul Phillips
Associate Production Editor: Will Moore
Senior Designer: Mark C. Kellogg
Senior Art Buyer: Alexandra F. Rockafellar
Photo Research: Paul Hahn
Production Manager: Abram Hall

Cover design by Mark C. Kellogg.
Cover photography by Brad Guice.

Illustrations and realia by: Kathryn Adams, Steve BonDurant/Icon
Graphics, Douglas Buchman, Todd Cooper, Dartmouth Publishing,
Sam Day, Hugh Harrison, Scott MacNeill, Karen Minot, Olivia,
Steve Stankiewicz, Chris Reed, William Waitzman, Rose
Zgodzinski.

Location photography by: Curt Fischer, Cynthia Hill, Ken Karp,
Dennis Kitchen, Stephen Ogilvy.

*The publisher would like to thank the following for their permission to
reproduce photography:* Rolf Adlercreutz/Liaison International, S.
Dooley/Liaison International, Michele and Tom Grimm/
International Stock Photo, R. Kord/H. Armstrong Roberts, John
Michael/International Stock, Dario Perla/International Stock Photo,
Tracy Pechette, H. Armstrong Roberts, James Seikin/Liaison
International, Michael Shay/FPG International, Superstock.

Printing (last digit): 20 19 18 17 16 15 14 13 12 11

Printed in Hong Kong.

The publisher wishes to thank the following for their help in
developing this new edition:
Ms. Charlotte Butler, Kanda Gaigo Gakuin, Tokyo; Ms. Toshiko Oi,
Kokusai Gaigo Senmon Gakko, Osaka; Mr. John Edwards, Sophia
University Community College, Tokyo; Mr. Phillip (PJ) McManus,
Sophia University Community College, Tokyo; Mr. Bill Roberson,
Aichi Kyoiku Daigaku (Aichi University of Education), Nagoya;
Ms. Kim Fine, Sumitomo Electric Industries, Osaka; Mr. Sean
McGovern, Setsunan University, Osaka; Mr. Kenneth Crown,
Tokyo Foreign Language College, Tokyo; Mr. Rory S. Baskin,
Koriyama Women's College, Koriyama; Mr. David Clay Dycus,
Aichi Shukutoku Junior College, Nagoya; Mr. Steve Mierzejewski,
Richard Scruggs, and Bob Mercier, IIST, Fujinomiya; Catherine
O'Keefe, OUP, Tokyo.

Sue Brioux Aldcorn wishes to thank the late Dr. Carlos A. Yorio,
Four Seasons Language School, the University of Toronto ESL
Program, and her husband, Skip. Special thanks to Shelagh Speers
of Oxford University Press and Kathy Sands Boehmer for their
suggestions, editorial expertise, and patience.

TO THE STUDENT

Up to now, your study of English has probably focused on the study of English grammar and vocabulary. You already know quite a lot about what the rules of English grammar are, and how to form sentences in English. This knowledge provides an important foundation for you, but it is not enough to enable you to speak English fluently. In order to develop conversational listening and speaking skills, you need practice in these skills, and this is what *New Person to Person* aims to give you.

The focus of each unit in *New Person to Person* is not grammar. Instead, each unit focuses on conversational tasks or functions such as introducing yourself, talking about likes and dislikes, inviting someone to go somewhere, and so on. In order to take part in English conversations, it is necessary to learn how these and other common functions are used in English.

New Person to Person gives you opportunities to listen to native speakers. It also gives you guided practice in using many conversational functions. This is done in the following way:

CONVERSATIONS

Every unit has two sections. Each section begins with a conversation that includes examples of the functions you will be studying in that section. Listen to them on the cassette or as your teacher reads them. You can use them to improve your understanding of spoken English and to hear the language used in both business and social situations.

GIVE IT A TRY

Each function that you hear in the conversation is presented separately. You will be able to concentrate on each one and practice it with a partner until you feel comfortable with it. You will also learn different ways to say the same thing and have the chance to practice using your own ideas.

LISTEN TO THIS

Both sections in each unit end with the opportunity for you to use what you have learned. You will hear conversations that will help you with real-life listening tasks such as finding out opening and closing times, getting directions, and listening to and writing down information on forms.

PERSON TO PERSON

At the end of each unit, you and your partner will work together to solve a problem based on the functions you have just learned. Each of you will have information that the other needs, so you will have to listen to and speak to each other carefully, often using ideas and opinions of your own.

We hope you will find that learning to speak and understand English is easier than you think. Like any skill, it involves practice. *New Person to Person* will guide you through various types of practice, moving from controlled to free use of the language. You can review what you have learned both within each unit and in special review units. The Let's Talk and Review Units at the end of the book provide you with the opportunity to use both the language and your imagination.

Because you will usually work with a partner, *New Person to Person* gives you as much conversational practice as is possible in a classroom situation. Remember, as you practice, that communication is more than just words: People "say" a lot with their faces, their bodies, and their tone of voice.

As you practice with your partner, don't keep your eyes "glued to the book." Instead, use the "read and look up" technique: Look at your line before you speak. Then immediately look at your partner, make eye contact, and say the line as if you were acting. You may look down at your lines as often as you need to, but look at your partner when you speak. This will improve your fluency.

In addition to the language presented in each unit, here are some expressions that will be very useful to you—both in and outside of class.

a. Please say that again.
b. I'm sorry. I don't understand.
c. Please speak more slowly.
d. How do you say _____ in English?

e. What does _____ mean?
f. I don't know.
g. May I ask a question?
h. How do you spell _____?

The speaking and listening practice you get in this book will give you a firm basis for using English outside the classroom and when talking to other speakers of English person to person.

CONTENTS

If you see someone you think you know, do you speak to them?
If yes, what questions can you ask?

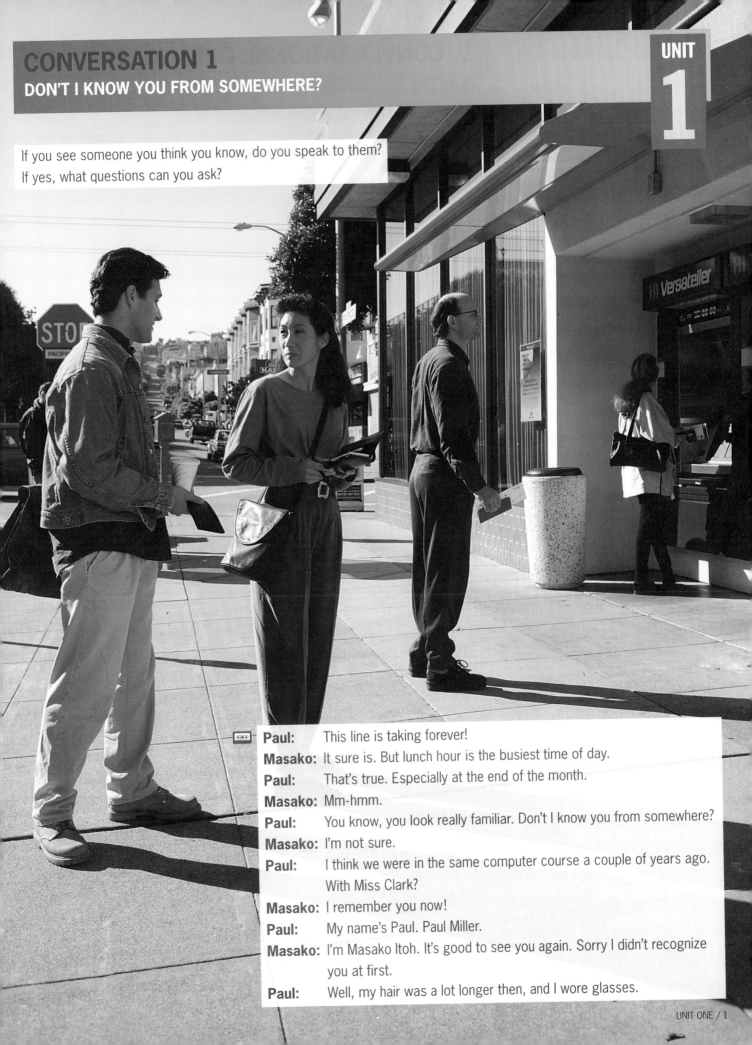

Paul:	This line is taking forever!
Masako:	It sure is. But lunch hour is the busiest time of day.
Paul:	That's true. Especially at the end of the month.
Masako:	Mm-hmm.
Paul:	You know, you look really familiar. Don't I know you from somewhere?
Masako:	I'm not sure.
Paul:	I think we were in the same computer course a couple of years ago. With Miss Clark?
Masako:	I remember you now!
Paul:	My name's Paul. Paul Miller.
Masako:	I'm Masako Itoh. It's good to see you again. Sorry I didn't recognize you at first.
Paul:	Well, my hair was a lot longer then, and I wore glasses.

1. CONVERSATIONAL OPENINGS

✦ This line is taking forever!
✧ It sure is. Lunch hour is the busiest time of day.

Practice 1

Start a conversation by choosing one of the openings below. Your partner answers with one of the responses below. Take turns.

Openings

1. I hope this course will be interesting.
2. Everything looks delicious. I don't know what to try first.
3. It's a beautiful wedding, isn't it?
4. I'm glad I came to this party. .

Responses

• Me, too. I'm having a great time.
• I think it will be. The professor is very good.
• It sure is. Mary Ann is a beautiful bride.
• Try the salmon. It's fantastic.

Practice 2

You and your partner are in the following situations. Take turns starting a conversation by using the cues below. Try to continue the conversation.

Example:
in a line at a movie
A: hope/good movie
B: newspaper review/excellent

Student A: I hope this is a good movie.
Student B: Well, the newspaper review was excellent.

1. at a party
A: think/great party
B: John's parties/always good

2. on the first day of class
B: heard/this teacher/very good
A: my older brother/really like her

3. at a baseball game
A: hope/Tigers win today
B: *your idea*

4. at the airport
B: can't wait/get to Hawaii
A: *your idea*

5. buying concert tickets
A: *your idea*
B: *your idea*

2. ASKING IF YOU'VE MET BEFORE

✦ Don't I know you from somewhere?
  Haven't we met before?

✧ I'm not sure. | Do you?
              | Have we?

✦ I think we *were in the same computer course.*
  You *were in my computer class, weren't you?*

✧ Oh, yes. I remember you now.
  Yes, that's right.
	✧ No, I don't think so.
	  I think you have the wrong person.

✦ My name's *Paul. Paul Miller.*	✦ Oh, sorry.
✧ I'm *Masako Itoh.*	

Practice 1

Student A: You see someone you think you know. You don't remember the person's name, but you think you remember something about him/her. Follow the model above, and check if you know him/her.

Cue: went to the same high school
Question: I think we went to the same high school.

Student B: Answer either *Yes, I remember you now* or *No, I don't think so.* Then reverse roles.

1. met at Kate Bowen's party
2. used to be neighbors
3. belong to the same tennis club
4. take the same train
5. *your idea*
6. *your idea*

Practice 2

Follow the instructions for Practice 1. This time, **Student B** checks if he/she knows them:

Cue: went to Milton High School
Question: You went to Milton High School, didn't you?

Student A answers either *Yes, that's right* or *No, I think you have the wrong person.*

1. work for IBM
2. studied at Harvard
3. are from Kyoto
4. are a teacher
5. *your idea*
6. *your idea*

LISTEN TO THIS

▭ Listen to the conversation and answer the questions below.

1. At first, does the man recognize the woman? ....
2. Where does the woman think the man's from? ....
3. Where does the woman think they met? ....
4. Have they met before? ....

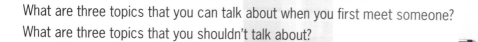

What are three topics that you can talk about when you first meet someone?
What are three topics that you shouldn't talk about?

Louis: Hi. Sorry I'm late.

Gina: Oh, that's OK. We just got here. Louis, this is my fiancé, Max. Max, this is my old friend, Louis. We went to school together.

Max: Hi, Louis. I'm really glad to meet you.

Louis: Hi, Max. I've heard a lot about you.

Max: All good, I hope!

Gina: Louis just got back from California.

Max: Really? How was it?

Louis: It was fantastic.

Gina: You went with your brother, didn't you?

Louis: Yeah. We saw a lot of California, that's for sure!

Max: I hear you like golf.

Louis: Love it! We played six different golf courses. Do you play?

Max: I sure do! How about a game this weekend?

Gina: Uh-oh. I was afraid of this.

Pronunciation Focus

Listen to the blended sounds in these words.

just got   meet you

about you   didn't you

Now practice the conversation. Pay attention to blended sounds.

1. MAKING SMALL TALK (1)

◆ I hear you like *golf*.

Do you	*play golf?*	
	like to go	*to art galleries?*
		fishing?

◇ Yes, I do. I love *golf*.	◇ No. I don't.
All the time.	Never.
Whenever I can.	I'm afraid I don't.
Sometimes.	

Practice 1

Ask your partner about the following activities. If he/she says yes, get more information by using the questions below or your own questions. Take turns asking about each activity.

1. ...go to concerts?   What kind of concerts?
                             Who's your favorite performer?

2. ...like to eat out?   What's your favorite restaurant?
                             What's your favorite food?

3. ...watch baseball?   What's your favorite team?
                             Who's your favorite player?

4. ...play any sports?   Which ones do you play?
                             Which one do you like best?

5. ...like to go to movies? *two of your ideas*

Practice 2

Now think of two activities that you enjoy. Move around the class and ask your classmates about them. If they answer yes, ask questions to get more information.

2. INTRODUCING FRIENDS

◆ *Louis*, this is (my fiancé,) *Max*. *Max*, this is *Louis*.

| ◇ I'm (really) glad | to meet you. |
| It's nice | |

◆ I'm glad	to meet you, too.
It's	nice	
	good	

Practice

In groups of three, introduce one friend to another. Use first names. Take turns making the introductions.

3. MAKING SMALL TALK (2)

✦ Louis just got back from California.

✧ (Really?) How was it?

| How long | were you | there? |
| | was he | |

| Which part did | you | visit? |
| | he | |

Practice

On a separate piece of paper, quickly write down:
1. something you did recently
2. the last place you visited
3. the last movie you saw
4. a hobby or sport that you like to do

Form a group of three. **Student A** introduces **Students B** and **C**. Then **Student A** uses one of the items **Student B** has written to begin the conversation. **Student C** continues the conversation by asking questions. Follow this model:

A: Yoko, this is my friend, Marge. Marge, this is Yoko.
B: Hi, Marge. It's nice to meet you.
C: It's good to meet you, too.
A: Yoko just graduated from college.
C: Really! What did you major in?
B: Music.

Change roles so that everyone has a chance to make the introductions and begin the conversation.

LISTEN TO THIS

▭ You are going to hear a conversation between two people who have just met. Read the question words below, then as you listen, put a check (✔) beside the types of questions the man asks. Finally, write down the main topic of the conversation.

☐ How ☐ Where ☐ What ☐ How far

☐ What time ☐ When ☐ Who ☐ Why

Main Topic [   ]

(Student A looks at this page. Student B looks at the next page.)

Practice 1

You are going to get to know a classmate by making small talk. Your partner should be someone that you don't know very well. Find out some things he/she likes to do. Ask questions to learn more and to continue the conversation. When you have finished talking, write down the things that your partner likes to do.

Student B likes...

Practice 2

Form a group of four. Introduce your partner to the group and report on something interesting you learned about your partner. Try to discover what things you all enjoy doing.

(Student B looks at this page. Student A looks at the previous page.)

Practice 1

You are going to get to know a classmate by making small talk. Your partner should be someone that you don't know very well. Find out some things he/she likes to do. Ask questions to learn more and to continue the conversation. When you have finished talking, write down the things that your partner likes to do.

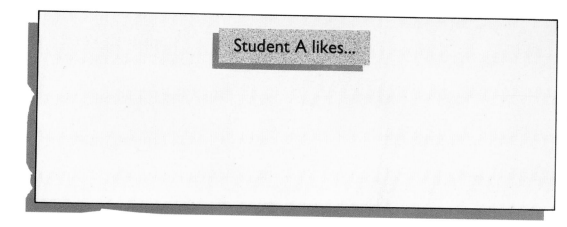

Student A likes...

Practice 2

Form a group of four. Introduce your partner to the group and report on something interesting you learned about your partner. Try to discover what things you all enjoy doing.

CONVERSATION 1
WHERE CAN YOU GET IT CLEANED?

Where do you think these men are going?
What is the man's problem?
Has something like this ever happened to you? What did you do?

Don: I'm glad you're here. What a terrible morning!

Neal: Why? What happened?

Don: After I got dressed for the wedding, I was having a cup of coffee, and I spilled it all over my shirt.

Neal: Well, it looks OK now.

Don: Luckily, I had another white shirt, so I changed.

Neal: Uh, Don, is there a place around here where you can get a pair of pants cleaned quickly?

Don: There's a one-hour dry cleaner in the Shell Building on Madison. It's about two blocks from here.

Neal: So, it's close. That's good. And which one is the Shell Building?

Don: It's that big, glass office building just past the park. But why all these questions about the dry cleaner?

Neal: Because we have to stop there on the way to the wedding. I think you sat in something.

Don: Oh, no!

1. ASKING WHERE SERVICES ARE LOCATED

✦ Where can | you | get *a pair of pants cleaned* around here?
| I | have *a watch fixed?*
| | mail *these letters?*

✧ (I think) there's a *dry cleaner* in *the Shell Building* on *Madison.*
You can go to the *jewelry store* at (the corner of) *Grant and Lee.*
There's a *post office* on *Lincoln Avenue.*

Practice 1

Student A: Ask your partner where you can get the following errands done.

1. your camera repaired
2. some photocopies made
3. a prescription filled

4. your jacket dry-cleaned
5. your passport picture taken
6. your hair cut

Student B: Check the map below and tell your partner the name of the place and its location.

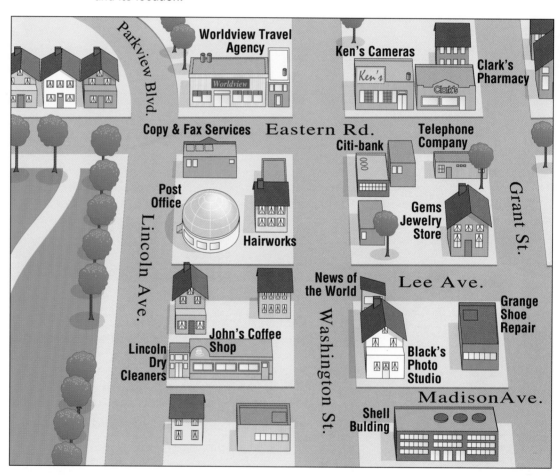

Practice 2

Student B: You want to do the following errands.

1. send a fax
2. mail a package
3. buy an airline ticket

4. buy a foreign newspaper
5. get pictures developed
6. change some money

Student A: Give the name and location of each place to your partner.

2. DESCRIBING BUILDINGS

✦ Which one is *the King Building?*

✧ It's	that the	*big, glass office building* (just)	past after before across from near next to	the park. the hotel.

Practice 1

Student A: Ask about four of the following buildings.
Student B: Describe the building and say where it is located.
Reverse roles and talk about the other four.

Student A
1. the King Building
2. Police Headquarters
3. the Planetarium
4. the Museum of Natural Science
5. the Grant Bank Tower
6. the Italian Embassy
7. the Shop-Rite Department Store
8. the City Reference Library

Student B
1. big, glass office building
2. low, red brick building
3. building with the domed roof
4. old, gray stone building
5. round glass tower
6. low, white building
7. large, red brick building
8. big, black office tower

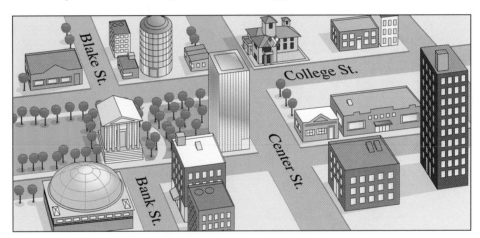

Practice 2

Take turns asking where you can get things done in your city. Use landmarks and streets to describe the locations.

LISTEN TO THIS

🔊 Listen to the conversation between Kumiko and her friend, Bruce.

1. What kind of store is Kumiko going to? ....
2. Write the letter of the building beside the correct name.

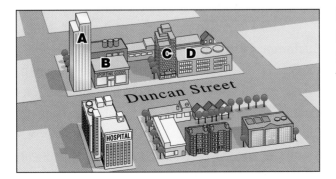

Metro Hotel ....

Manulife Building ....

Manning Building ....

The Sports Shop ....

What is this woman's job?

What questions do you think people ask her?

Clerk: Next, please!

Customer #1: Could you tell me where the toy department is?

Clerk: The toy department is on the fourth floor.... Next?

Customer #2: Where can I exchange this computer game?

Clerk: You can do that in Electronics on five.... Can I help you?

Customer #3: I'm looking for ladies' gloves.

Clerk: Ladies' gloves are here on the main floor. Walk down this aisle to the scarf counter. Turn left. They're just past the handbags.

Customer #4: Is there a pharmacy in this mall?

Clerk: Yes, there is. Just walk down there past the fountain. The pharmacy is about four stores down from there on your left.

Customer #4: Thank you.

Clerk: Yes, sir?

Customer #5: Where can I watch TV while my friends are shopping?

Pronunciation Focus

Listen to the consonant clusters in these words.

exchange	electronics	gloves
scarf	left	past
handbags	friends	department

Now practice the conversation. Pay attention to the consonant clusters.

1. ASKING FOR DIRECTIONS IN A STORE (1)

✦ Could you tell me where *the toy department* is?
Where can I *exchange this computer game?*

✧ The *toy department* is on the fourth floor.
You can do that in *Electronics on five.*

Practice 1

Student A: You are at the information desk of a large department store.
Student B: Use the information in the directory to answer.

Student A wants:

1. to go to children's wear
2. to pay his/her account
3. to go to the furniture department
4. to exchange a man's sweater
5. *your idea*

Practice 2

Reverse roles. This time **Student A** answers.

Student B wants:

1. to go to ladies' wear
2. to look at men's suits
3. to have lunch
4. to go to the jewelry department
5. *your idea*

FIELDS DEPARTMENT STORE

Accessories	Main
Appliances	5
Children's wear	3
Credit office	5
Electronics	5
Furniture	4
Jewelry	Main
Ladies' wear	2
Men's wear	2
Restaurant	5
Rest rooms	3, 5
Toys	4

2. ASKING FOR DIRECTIONS IN A STORE (2)

✦ I'm looking for *gloves for my sister.*

✧ *Ladies' gloves are here on the main floor. Walk down this aisle to the scarf counter. Turn left. They're just past the handbags.*

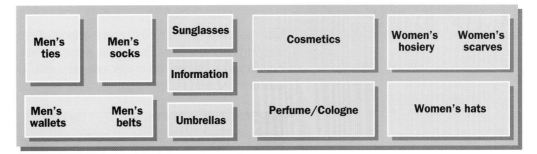

Men's ties	Men's socks	Sunglasses	Cosmetics	Women's hosiery	Women's scarves
Men's wallets	Men's belts	Information	Perfume/Cologne	Women's hats
		Umbrellas		

Practice

Take turns asking about where things are located on the main floor. Choose from the list below and add three ideas of your own. You are at the information desk.

- an umbrella
- cosmetics
- a pair of sunglasses
- a scarf for my grandmother
- a tie for my father
- men's socks

3. ASKING FOR DIRECTIONS IN A MALL

✦ Is there *a pharmacy* in this mall?
Where can I buy *some toothpaste* around here?

✧ Walk past the | *fountain.*
| *camera store.*

The pharmacy is about | *four* | stores down on your | *left.*
| *six* | | *right.*

Practice

Take turns asking and answering questions about where things are in the mall. Choose from the lists below.

Type of store
a tape and CD store
a bookstore
a children's shoe store
an adult shoe store
a hair salon
your ideas

Type of purchase
some sheets and pillowcases
a new pair of jeans
some jewelry
some wrapping paper and a card
some film for your camera
your ideas

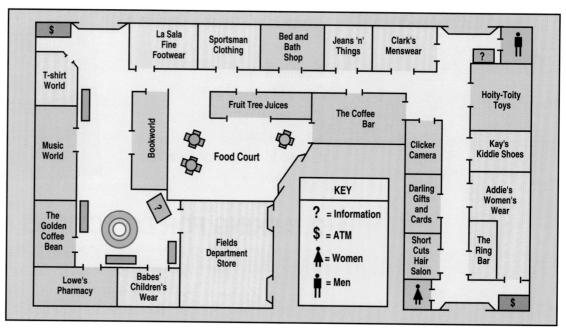

LISTEN TO THIS

📼 You will hear three customers asking where they can find various departments in a large downtown store. Listen and write down the number of the conversation beside the correct department. Then write the floor number the customer should go to.

Conversation Number	Store Directory	Floor Number
	Appliances	
	Furniture	
	Garden Shop	
	Sporting goods	

(Student A looks at this page. Student B looks at the next page.)

It is December, and you are going shopping for gifts. Think of four people you want to get something for. They can be relatives, friends, a teacher, or your boss. Write down their names and the gift you would most like to give them.

Name	Gift
....	....
....	....
....	....
....	....

Practice 1

Ask your partner for the name of the best place to get each of the four gifts you listed above. Be sure to get exact locations. Start like this:

A: What's the best place to get *a bicycle* for *my little brother?*
B: I think the best place is ....

Practice 2

Now your partner will ask you where he/she can buy some gifts. Give the name of the place you think is best, and describe exactly how to get there.

PERSON TO PERSON

STUDENT B

(Student B looks at this page. Student A looks at the previous page.)

It is December, and you are going shopping for gifts. Think of four people you want to get something for. They can be relatives, friends, a teacher, or your boss. Write down their names and the gift you would most like to give them.

Name	Gift
....	....
....	....
....	....
....	....

Practice 1

Your partner will ask you where he/she can buy some gifts. Give the name of the place you think is best, and describe exactly how to get there. Start like this:

A: What's the best place to get *a bicycle* for *my little brother*?
B: I think the best place is ....

Practice 2

Now ask your partner for the name of the best place to get each of the four gifts you listed above. Be sure to get exact locations.

On the phone, do you prefer to leave messages or call back later?
What information should you give when you leave a message?

Helen:	Hello?
Danny:	Hello. Could I please speak to Helen?
Helen:	Speaking.
Danny:	Hi, Helen. This is Danny. Listen, I'm having a party at my place this Friday night. Are you free?
Helen:	Sure! What time?
Danny:	Anytime after 8:00.
Helen:	Great! See you Friday, then.

Mrs. King:	Hello?
Danny:	Hi, Mrs. King. Is John there, please?
Mrs. King:	I'm sorry he's not here right now. Could I take a message?
Danny:	Yes, please. I'm calling to tell him there's a party at my place on Friday, and…
Mrs. King:	Let me get a pen. All right, go ahead.
Danny:	OK, this is Danny Silver, and my number is 364-0107. Could you ask him to call me at home? I can give him all the details then.
Mrs. King:	Sure. I'll give him the message as soon as he gets in. I'll tell him to call Danny at 364-0107.
Danny:	Thanks. Good-bye.

1. ASKING TO SPEAK TO SOMEONE

◆ Hello?

◇ Hi. Could I please speak to *Helen*?

◆ Speaking.

◇ Hi, *Helen*. This is *Danny*.

◆ Hello?

◇ Hi. Is *Helen* there, please?

◆ Sure. Just a | moment | please.
          | minute |
Hold on. I'll get *her*.

Practice

Call your partner. Follow each of the models above. Reverse roles.

2. OFFERING TO TAKE A MESSAGE

◆ I'm sorry, | *he's not here right now.*
          | *he can't come to the phone right now.*
Could | I take a message?
Can |

◇ No thanks. I'll call back.
Yes, please.

Practice 1

Student A: Call a friend.
Student B: Answer and say that the friend is not available. Use the cues below to explain. Start like this:

B: Hello?

A: Hello. Could I please speak to ....?

B: I'm sorry,...

Student B's cues

1. he/she is out for the evening

2. he/she won't be back until 6:00

3. he/she isn't home yet

Practice 2

Reverse roles. This time **Student B** is calling and **Student A** explains.

Student A's cues

1. he/she is out of town for a week

2. he/she has gone to see a movie

3. he/she will be home in half an hour

Practice 3

Choose a new partner. Follow the instructions for Practices 1 and 2, but this time use all your own ideas.

3. WRITING MESSAGES DOWN

◆ Let me get a pen. All right, go ahead.

◇ Could you | ask him to | call | *Danny* | at home?
              | have him | | *me* | when he gets in?

This is *Danny Silver*, and my number is *364-0107*.

I'm calling to tell | *John* | there's a party at my place on Friday.
Please tell | *him* | I'll pick him up at 6:30.

◆ OK. I'll tell him to call *Danny Silver* at *364-0107*.

Practice 1

Student A: You are calling a friend, Gina.
Student B: Offer to take a message. Write it down on a separate piece of paper, and repeat it back to **Student A**.
(**Student A:** Don't forget to leave your name and number.)

Start like this:

A: Could I please speak to Gina?

B: Sorry, she's out right now. Could I take a message?

A: Yes, please.

B: Let me get a pen…

Student A's messages

1. call me when she gets back

2. call me about tonight's homework

3. can't pick her up in the morning

Practice 2

Follow the instructions for Practice 1, but this time **Student B** is calling.

Student B's messages

1. need to talk about our plans for this Saturday

2. call me back before midnight

3. need Mark's new telephone number

Practice 3

Call your partner to leave a message for someone. Your partner will repeat the message back to you. Use your own ideas. Reverse roles.

LISTEN TO THIS

Listen to the following phone calls. Write down the details of each call below.

Who called:
_____

Phone number:
_____

Message: _____
_____
_____

Who called: _____
Phone number: _____

Message:
_____
_____
_____

I'M SORRY. HER LINE IS BUSY RIGHT NOW.

What are the advantages of studying English abroad?
What are some of the difficulties of studying abroad?

Voice: You have reached the English Language Institute. If you have a Touch-Tone phone, and you want the Admissions Office, press 1 now. For General Information, press 2 now. If you know…

Secretary: Good morning. Admissions Office. Can I help you?

Manuel: Yes, please. My nephew in Mexico is interested in taking your course. I'm calling to find out how he can apply.

Secretary: We just need a completed application form and the registration fee.

Manuel: Where can I find out about student housing?

Secretary: From Ms. Sharma in the General Information Office.

Manuel: Could I speak to Ms. Sharma, please?

Secretary: Of course. Hold the line, please.— I'm sorry, her line is busy right now.

Manuel: Could I leave a message for her?

Secretary: Certainly.

Manuel: My name is Manuel Varga. V-A-R-G-A. My number is 493-2542. I want to find out about residence fees. Can she call me back?

Secretary: Yes. I'll give her the message.

Manuel: Thank you.

Pronunciation Focus

Listen to the stress on these words.

1st syllable	2nd syllable	3rd syllable
language	admissions	information
institute	apply	application
interested	completed	registration

Now practice the conversation. Pay attention to stressed syllables.

1. ASKING TO SPEAK TO SOMEONE

♦ Could I | speak to *Ms. Sharma*, please?
           | have the *General Information Office*?
Is *Ms. Sharma* available, please?

✧ Hold the line, please.
One moment, please.
I'll see if *she's* available.

I'm sorry. | *Her line is busy* right now.
           | *She's* | on another line now.
                     | not in the office today.

Practice

Student A: You have business calls to make.
Student B: Use the cues below, and follow the model above.
Then reverse roles.

Student A's cues
1. Ms. Johnson
2. Mr. Ferguson
3. Repair Department
4. Accounts Office

Student B's cues
1. out for lunch
2. on another line
3. one moment
4. line is busy

2. LEAVING A MESSAGE

♦ Could I leave a message for | her?
                               | him?

✧ Certainly.

♦ My name is *Manuel Varga*. *V-A-R-G-A*. My number is *493-2542*. I want
to find out about *residence fees*. Can *she* please call me back?

Practice 1

Student A: You need to speak to Ms. Sharma to get the following information.
Ask to leave a message. Use your own name and number.
Student B: Explain why Ms. Sharma can't take the call. Cover **A's** information
and take a message. Use the message pads below.

A's messages: 1. received my application yet
2. when I can move into the dormitory

Practice 2

Reverse roles and follow the instructions for Practice 1.
Student A: Cover **B's** information and take messages using the message pads.

B's messages: 1. have a problem with my class schedule
2. can change to a higher level class
Example:

Message for: _Ms. Sharma_
Message from: _Manuel Varga_
Telephone number: _493-2542_
Message: _to find out about residence fees_
Please call back. ✓

Message for: _____
Message from: _____
Telephone number: _____
Message: _____

Message for: _____
Message from: _____
Telephone number: _____
Message: _____
Please call back. ☐

3. CALLING FOR INFORMATION

◆ Can I help you?

◇ Yes, please. | *How does my nephew apply?*
When do I pay my fees?
Are there any social activities?

Practice 1

Student A: Your partner is the Social Director for your class at the English Language Institute. Call him/her for the information below. Follow this model:

Student A's cue: are there/activities/this month?
Student B's cue: yes/weekend trip/potluck dinner

A: Are there any activities for this month?
B: Yes. There's a weekend trip and a potluck dinner.

Student A wants to know	Student B's information
1. where/weekend trip?	1. Washington, D.C.
2. when/weekend trip?	2. May 15th to May 17th
3. how/get there?	3. by bus
4. *your question*	4. *your idea*
5. *your question*	5. *your idea*

Practice 2

Student B: Follow the instructions for Practice 1, but this time your partner is the Social Director, and you want information about the potluck dinner.

Student B wants to know	Student A's information
1. when/party	1. Saturday night
2. where/party	2. Diana's house
3. who/going	3. your class
4. *your question*	4. *your idea*
5. *your question*	5. *your idea*

LISTEN TO THIS

You will hear four people making business calls. As you listen, fill in the chart below. If the person, office, or department is not available, fill in the reason. The first one is done for you.

Place called	Available?	Why not?
1. University of Miami	no	Lines are busy.
2. Medical Clinic		
3. Computer City		
4. Global Travel		

(Student A looks at this page. Student B looks at the next page.)

Margo is the receptionist at a large record company. She answers the phone for three busy executives. Below are their schedules for this afternoon.

Practice 1

Listen as Margo answers the phone, and fill in the empty squares with the appropriate information.

	1:00 PM	2:00 PM	3:00 PM	4:00 PM
Ed Black	lunch with The Music Demons		audition new bands	party at Sheraton Hotel
Sara Brown	out to lunch	visit the recording studio	in a press conference	
Liz White	lunch with Roberto Moti	back at 2:30	meetings with lawyers	out of the office

Practice 2

You are the receptionist at Star-Struck Records. Use the chart above to answer **Student B's** call. Offer to take a message.
The time of Student B's call is 2:15 PM.

MESSAGES

Message for:

Message from:

Telephone number:

Message:

Please call back. ☐

Repeat the message to make sure you have it correct.

Practice 3

Student B is the receptionist at Star-Struck Records. You call and want to speak to Ed Black. The message is that his wife has gone to the hospital to have the baby, and he should go there as soon as possible. Use your own name and phone number.
The time of your call is 4:30 PM.

(Student B looks at this page. Student A looks at the previous page.)

Margo is the receptionist at a large record company. She answers the phone for three busy executives. Below are their schedules for this afternoon.

Practice 1

Listen as Margo answers the phone, and fill in the empty squares with the appropriate information.

	1:00 PM	2:00 PM	3:00 PM	4:00 PM
Ed Black	lunch with The Music Demons	on a long-distance call to Paris	audition new bands	
Sara Brown	out to lunch	visit the recording studio	in a press conference	her line is busy
Liz White	lunch with Roberto Moti		meetings with lawyers	out of the office

Practice 2

Student A is the receptionist at Star-Struck Records. You call and want to speak to Liz White. The message is that you have to cancel your appointment on Thursday. You would like Liz White to call you so you can arrange a new time. Use your own name and phone number.

The time of your call is 2:15 PM.

Practice 3

You are the receptionist at Star-Struck Records. Use the chart above to answer your partner's call. Offer to take a message.

The time of Student A's call is 4:30 PM.

MESSAGES

Message for:
Message from:
Telephone number:
Message: Please call back. ☐

Repeat the message to make sure you have it correct.

Do you know any smokers?
How do you feel about smoking?

Glen: That was my mother on the phone. She and my father will be here Friday.

Gail: Yeah…

Glen: What's the matter? Don't you like them?

Gail: Sure I do! It's their smoking I don't like. I really don't want them to smoke in the house.

Glen: They're just here for the weekend. It's not a big problem, is it?

Gail: Second-hand smoke is a big problem around here. It's dangerous— especially for the baby. Besides, everything stinks for a week!

Glen: I know what you mean. But what can we do?

Gail: We can ask them to smoke outside.

Glen: I guess you're right. OK. You can tell them when they get here.

Gail: Me? Are you kidding? They're your parents! You tell them!

1. IDENTIFYING A PROBLEM

✦ *Second-hand smoke* is a big problem *around here.*

✧ I know what you mean. | It's *dangerous.*
You're (absolutely) right. |

Practice 1

Look at the pictures below. Then, with your partner, choose phrases from below to say *why* it is a problem.

- difficult to breathe
- bad for the environment
- ugly to look at

- unhealthy
- dangerous for wildlife
- difficult to enjoy a meal

smoking in restaurants

water pollution

too many cars

littering

Practice 2

With your partner, identify a problem in your city, a problem in your country, and a problem in the world. Say why each one is a problem. A few common problems are listed below.

City: crime, overcrowding, cost of living, not enough parks

Country: high taxes, weak government, unemployment

World: war, overpopulation, racism, starvation, terrorism

Start like this:

.... is a big problem in this city.

.... in this country.

.... in the world.

Practice 3

In a small group or as a class, discuss the three problems you and your partner identified.

2. MAKING SUGGESTIONS

✦ What can we do?
  What can we do about *second-hand smoke*?

✧ We can ask them to | *smoke outside.*
  They could |

Practice 1

This time, discuss the problem of too many cars in the city with your partner. Use the suggestions below or your own ideas. Follow this model:

A: I think there are too many cars in this city.
B: You're absolutely right. It's hard to breathe downtown.
A: But what can we do?
B: *your suggestion*
A: Or,...*your suggestion*

Suggestions
- provide more efficient public transportation
- encourage people to ride bicycles
- arrange car pools
- make gasoline more expensive

Practice 2

In a small group, choose one of the problems identified on the previous page. Ask for and make suggestions to solve the problem. Follow the model for Practice 1.

LISTEN TO THIS

🔊 A spokesperson is discussing ways that people can help save the environment. She will talk about things that can be done around the home and in the community. As you listen, check (✔) the suggestions that she actually mentions.

Around the home	In the community
.........Buy cloth napkins	.... Ride a bicycle
.........Buy overpackaged goods	.... Get your office to recycle paper
.......Take bags to the grocery store	.... Teach young children to recycle
.........Use homemade cleaning products	.... Plant a tree

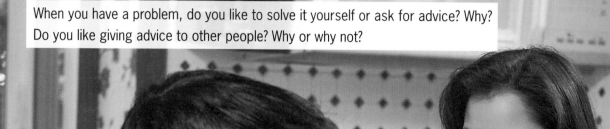

CONVERSATION 2
WHAT WOULD YOU DO?

When you have a problem, do you like to solve it yourself or ask for advice? Why?
Do you like giving advice to other people? Why or why not?

John: OK, Beth, what's the problem? Do you want to talk about it?

Beth: No… Yes… I don't know.

John: Come on, Beth, I'm your brother — what's the matter?

Beth: It's Ken. He's really fun to be with, but he's the cheapest guy I've ever gone out with.

John: Why? What did he do?

Beth: Last night we went to a movie. I bought the tickets while he parked the car.

John: So?

Beth: Well, he never gave me any money for his ticket. And you won't believe what happened next!

John: Yeah?

Beth: He went to the snack bar and came back with popcorn and a soda… for himself! He never even asked me if I wanted anything!

John: Wow! That sounds pretty bad.

Beth: I know. I really like him, but he makes me mad, too. What should I do?

John: You should start looking for a new boyfriend!

Pronunciation Focus

Words that are stressed in sentences are usually the words that carry important meaning in the sentence. Listen to the stressed words.

Whát's the próblem?

Whát did he dó?

Now listen to the conversation again and mark the stressed words. Then practice the conversation.

ASKING FOR AND GIVING ADVICE

◆ What's the | problem? | Do you want to talk about it?
| matter? |

◇ *Ken is the cheapest guy I've ever gone out with.*
I really like Ken, but he makes me mad.

What | should | I do?
| can |
What would you do?
I don't know what to do.

◆ You should | *start looking* | for a new boyfriend.
Why don't you | *look* |

Practice 1

Student A: Your partner seems upset. Find out what his/her problem is. Choose the best advice from the suggestions below or use your own ideas.
Student B: Explain your problem and ask for advice.

Student B's problems

1. your math grades are very poor

2. you share a room with your brother/sister and he/she snores

3. you're getting fat; your clothes don't fit

4. you saw your boyfriend/girlfriend holding hands with someone else

Student A's suggestions

• wake him/her up
• ask him/her about it
• start exercising
• buy some earplugs

• go on a diet
• study more
• break up with him/her
• ask for extra help

Practice 2

Follow the instructions for Practice 1. This time **Student A** has the problem.

Student A's problems

1. your brother/sister takes your things without asking

2. your best friend owes you money

3. you are always tired in class

4. your parents are too strict

Student B's suggestions

• tell your parents how you feel
• go to bed earlier
• take something of his/hers
• ask the friend to lend you money

• ask him/her to pay you back
• tell your parents
• drink coffee before class
• ask your parents to change
their rules

Make a group of four students. Each of you will describe an everyday problem and get advice from the other members of your group. Write down the best advice. Start like this:

A: I have a problem and I don't know what to do....

Student A's problem

"I've had the same job for five years. I'm really bored with it."

Best Advice ....

Student B's problem

"My parents don't like my boyfriend/girlfriend, but I'm madly in love with him/her."

Best Advice ....

Student C's problem

"I told my best friend a secret and he/she told everybody. Now I can't trust him/her anymore."

Best Advice ....

Student D's problem

"My housemate is really messy. He/she always leaves a mess and won't do any housework."

Best Advice ....

LISTEN TO THIS

You will hear people asking their friends for advice. As you listen, write the number of the problem next to the advice that the friend gives.

Problem	Advice
1. can't go to the party	.... learn to live with it
2. daughter wants her own apartment	.... say no
3. friend doesn't return things	.... promise to come home early

(Student A looks at this page. Student B looks at the next page.)

▭ "The Problem Panel" is a call-in radio talk show. People call and tell their problems to two experts, Dr. Joseph Fields and Dr. Joan Burke, who give them advice. Listen, as Gloria calls with a problem.

Practice 1

Write down Gloria's problem.

....

....

....

Write down Dr. Fields' advice.

....

....

....

Practice 2

Your partner will tell you the advice that Gloria received from Dr. Burke. Tell your partner the advice Gloria received from Dr. Fields. Discuss both and decide which expert made the best suggestion.

Practice 3

Now you and your partner are experts. Imagine that Gloria is calling you, and make your own suggestions. Share your ideas with other pairs or with the class.

(Student B looks at this page. Student A looks at the previous page.)

"The Problem Panel" is a call-in radio talk show. People call and tell their problems to two experts, Dr. Joseph Fields and Dr. Joan Burke, who give them advice. Listen, as Gloria calls with a problem.

Practice 1

Write down Gloria's problem.

....

....

....

Write down Dr. Burke's advice.

....

....

....

Practice 2

Your partner will tell you the advice that Gloria received from Dr. Fields. Tell your partner the advice Gloria received from Dr. Burke. Discuss both and decide which expert made the best suggestion.

Practice 3

Now you and your partner are experts. Imagine that Gloria is calling you, and make your own suggestions. Share your ideas with other pairs or with the class.

When you meet an old friend, what do you talk about?
Is it usual to talk about other old friends?

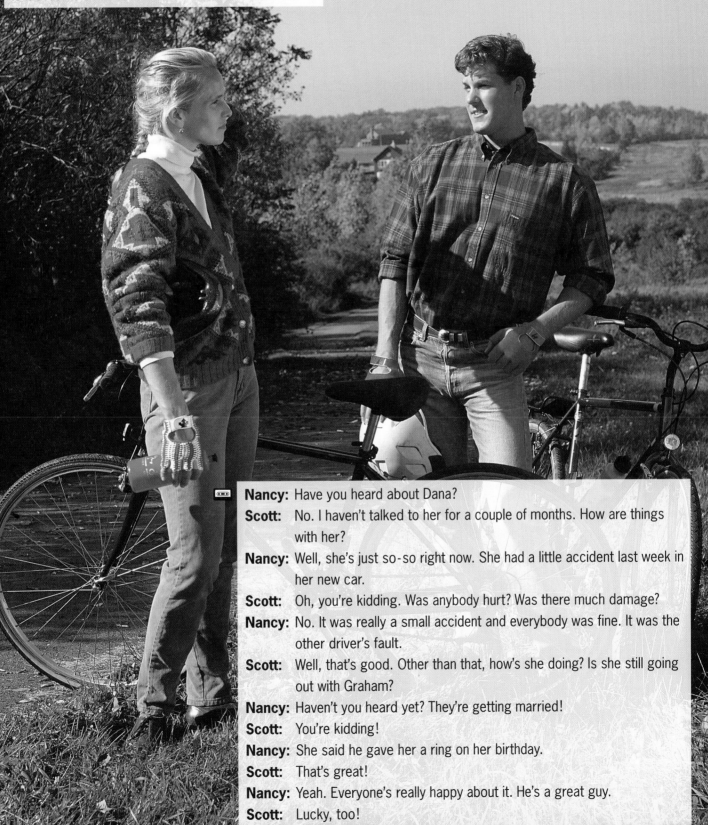

Nancy: Have you heard about Dana?

Scott: No. I haven't talked to her for a couple of months. How are things with her?

Nancy: Well, she's just so-so right now. She had a little accident last week in her new car.

Scott: Oh, you're kidding. Was anybody hurt? Was there much damage?

Nancy: No. It was really a small accident and everybody was fine. It was the other driver's fault.

Scott: Well, that's good. Other than that, how's she doing? Is she still going out with Graham?

Nancy: Haven't you heard yet? They're getting married!

Scott: You're kidding!

Nancy: She said he gave her a ring on her birthday.

Scott: That's great!

Nancy: Yeah. Everyone's really happy about it. He's a great guy.

Scott: Lucky, too!

1. ASKING ABOUT OTHER PEOPLE

✦ How is *Dana* (doing)? How are things with *Dana*?	✧ She's	great. pretty good. so-so. not bad. not too good.

✦ What's happening with	*Dana?* *her?*	✧ *She and Graham are getting married.* *She had a little accident.*
What's *she* doing these days?		

Practice

Take turns asking and answering about the people below. Follow this model, using the cues.

A: How's Dana doing?
B: She's so-so.
A: What's happening with her?
B: She had a little accident.

Cues
• broke her leg
• got engaged
• wife had twins
• had a car accident

2. GIVING INFORMATION ABOUT OTHER PEOPLE

✦ Have you heard	about *Dana?*
Did you hear	
Did I tell you	

✧ No.	How are things with *her?*
	How's *she* doing these days?
	What happened?

✦ *She's so-so. She had an accident in her new car.*

Give your partner information about two of these people. Use the model on the previous page and the cues below. Reverse roles and talk about the other two.

Cues
- graduated first in her class
- bought a new house
- ran over his daughter's bike
- didn't get the job he wanted

WANDA   FERNANDO   SAM   YUMI

Practice 2

Follow the instructions for Practice 1, but use your own ideas.
Start like this: "Have you heard about (name of classmate)?"

3. REACTING TO GOOD AND BAD NEWS

✦ They're getting married.	✦ She had an accident.
✧ Really? You're kidding! That's great! I'm really happy to hear that.	✧ Oh, no! You're kidding. That's too bad. I'm sorry to hear that.

Practice 1

Choose situations from the practices you have already done. This time react positively or negatively to the news. Use the pictures as cues.

Practice 2

Think of a famous person who has been in the news recently. Ask your partner what's happening with him/her. React honestly. Then reverse roles.

LISTEN TO THIS

You will hear three conversations. Put the number of the conversation beside the correct picture. Below each picture, write whether the person hearing the news thought it was good or bad.

....

Do you think most people like to gossip?
What kind of people like to gossip?

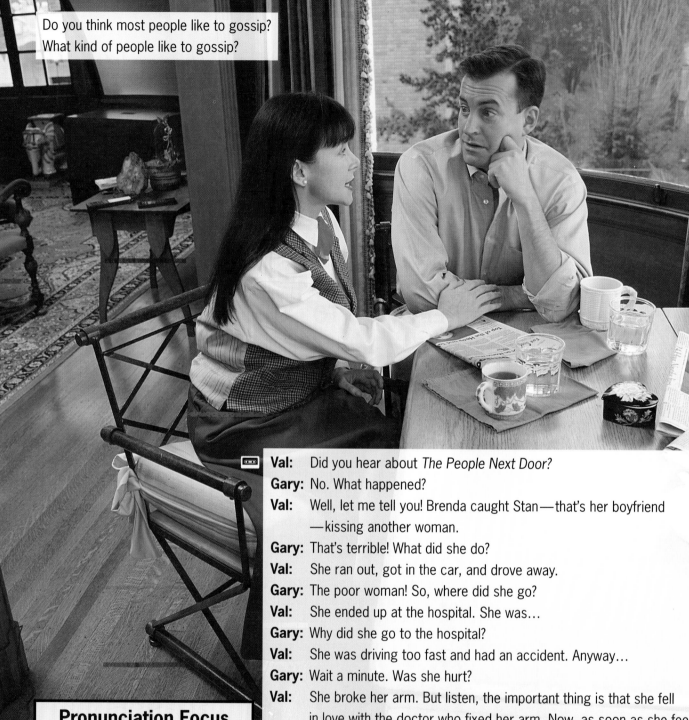

Val: Did you hear about *The People Next Door?*

Gary: No. What happened?

Val: Well, let me tell you! Brenda caught Stan—that's her boyfriend—kissing another woman.

Gary: That's terrible! What did she do?

Val: She ran out, got in the car, and drove away.

Gary: The poor woman! So, where did she go?

Val: She ended up at the hospital. She was…

Gary: Why did she go to the hospital?

Val: She was driving too fast and had an accident. Anyway…

Gary: Wait a minute. Was she hurt?

Val: She broke her arm. But listen, the important thing is that she fell in love with the doctor who fixed her arm. Now, as soon as she feels a little better, they're going to start dating.

Gary: Let me get this straight. Brenda caught Stan with another woman, got into a car accident, and now she's going out with her doctor?

Val: That's right.

Gary: That's unbelievable. It sounds like a soap opera.

Val: Gary. It *is* a soap opera. It's called *The People Next Door.* It's on TV every day at noon.

Pronunciation Focus

Listen to the stressed and unstressed
words in these sentences.

Let mé tell yóu.   What díd she dó?

Where díd she gó?   Wás she húrt?

Now practice the conversation. Notice
the difference between the stressed and
unstressed words.

1. ASKING FOR MORE DETAILS

◆ What did *she* do?
✧ *She ran out, got in the car, and drove away.*

◆ Where did *she* go?
✧ *She ended up in the hospital.*

◆ When *are they going to start dating?*
✧ *As soon as she feels a little better*

Practice 1

Student A: Tell **Student B** what happened to your friend, Henry.
Student B: Get details by asking a *what*, a *where*, and a *when* question.
Student A: Answer by choosing from the lists below. There are many possible answers.
Follow this model:

A: Did you hear about *my friend, Henry?*
B: No. What happened?
A: *He found a $100 bill.*
B: That's great! Where?
A: *In the park.*
B: When did he find it?
A: It was *late last night.*

What	**Where**	**When**
found a $100 bill	with Sony	about two weeks ago
won a singing contest	at the film festival	yesterday morning
got a new puppy	in the park	late last night
met a movie star	at the pet store	last month sometime
got a great job	at the karaoke club	last week
your idea	*your idea*	*your idea*

Practice 2

Reverse roles. **Student B** tells what happened to his/her friend, Penny.

Practice 3

Student A: Think of something interesting that happened to someone you know. Tell your partner.
Student B: Ask questions to get more details.

2. INTERRUPTING FOR DETAILS

◆ Wait | a minute.
  Just | a second.
  Hold on (a minute).
         (a second).

Why did she go to the hospital?
◇ *She had a car accident.*
◆ *Was she hurt?*
◇ *She broke her arm.*
◆ *When did this happen?*
◇ *About three weeks ago.*

Practice

Make a group of four students. One of you begins a story. The others in your group interrupt and ask questions to get more details. Continue in this way until no one can think of any more questions. Each student in the group takes a turn as the storyteller. Choose from the cues below or use your own ideas.

Story Cues

• uncle got an award from the mayor

• little brother was on television last night

• cousin ran away to get married

• neighbor went to Alaska

• uncle sold his new Rolls Royce for $10

Example:
Cue: uncle got an award from the mayor
Student A: My uncle got an award from the mayor.
Student B: Wait a minute. Why did he get an award?
Student A: He saved a little boy.

LISTEN TO THIS

John is the head of a university. He is telling his wife, Gwen, about what happened today. She asks him several questions in order to get more details. Briefly, write John's answers to Gwen's questions.

1. What happened? ....

2. Who is Hector Rojas? ....

3. How much is the grant worth? ....

4. What will it be used for? ....

PERSON TO PERSON

STUDENT A

(Student A looks at this page. Student B looks at the next page.)

Lucy and Ken are a married couple. They have some decisions to make. This morning, Lucy was talking to her friend, Jean, about them. Ken was talking to his friend, Stuart, about the decisions, too. Now, Jean and Stuart are talking about Lucy and Ken.

Practice 1

Listen to Jean and Stuart's conversation. Write down Jean's news about Lucy and her house, her son, and her job.

Her house	Her son	Her job

Practice 2

Discuss the following with your partner:

What problem do Ken and Lucy have?

Do you think this is a problem? Why or why not?

What do you think they should do?

(Student B looks at this page. Student A looks at the previous page.)

📼 Lucy and Ken are a married couple. They have some decisions to make. This morning, Lucy was talking to her friend, Jean, about them. Ken was talking to his friend, Stuart, about the decisions, too. Now, Jean and Stuart are talking about Lucy and Ken.

Practice 1

Listen to Jean and Stuart's conversation. Write down Stuart's news about Ken's job offer.

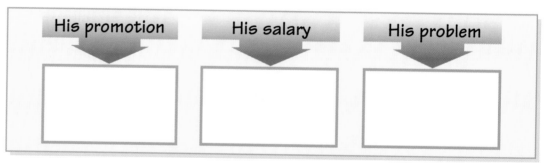

His promotion	His salary	His problem

Practice 2

Discuss the following with your partner:

What problem do Ken and Lucy have?

Do you think this is a problem? Why or why not?

What do you think they should do?

CONVERSATION 1
I FEEL TERRIBLE.

What do you think is wrong with this man?
What do you do when you have the flu?

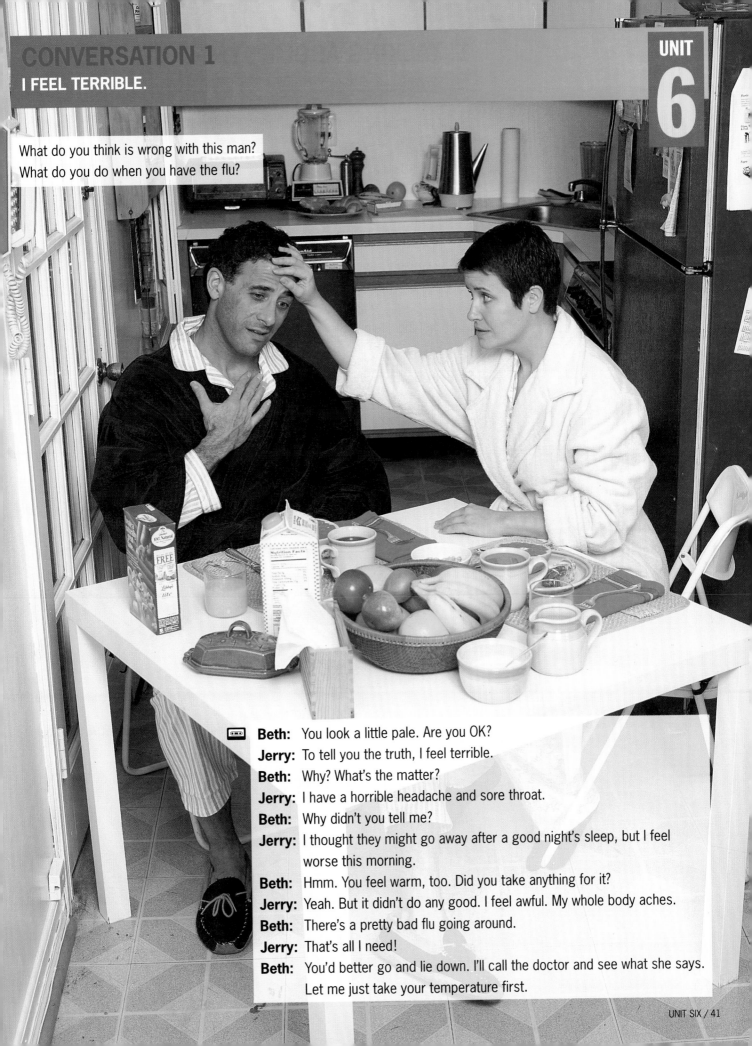

Beth: You look a little pale. Are you OK?

Jerry: To tell you the truth, I feel terrible.

Beth: Why? What's the matter?

Jerry: I have a horrible headache and sore throat.

Beth: Why didn't you tell me?

Jerry: I thought they might go away after a good night's sleep, but I feel worse this morning.

Beth: Hmm. You feel warm, too. Did you take anything for it?

Jerry: Yeah. But it didn't do any good. I feel awful. My whole body aches.

Beth: There's a pretty bad flu going around.

Jerry: That's all I need!

Beth: You'd better go and lie down. I'll call the doctor and see what she says. Let me just take your temperature first.

1. TALKING ABOUT SYMPTOMS

✦ Are you OK?

✧ To tell you the truth, | I feel terrible.
| I don't feel very well.

✦ What's the matter?

✧ I have | *a headache.*
| *a sore throat.*
| *a pain in my back.*

✦ Oh, I'm sorry to hear that.

Practice 1

Tell your partner that you're not feeling well. Answer your partner's questions, using the cues below. Start like this:

Student A: I don't feel very well today.
Student B: Why? What's the matter?

Cues

1. a fever
2. a bad cold
3. a backache
4. a toothache

5. an allergy
6. stiff muscles
7. a sore throat
8. insomnia

Practice 2

Reverse roles. This time **Student B** doesn't feel well, and **Student A** finds out what's wrong.

2. GIVING ADVICE

✧ I have *a headache.*

✦ I'm sorry to hear that. | Did you *take any aspirin?*
| You should *take an aspirin.*
| You'd better *go and lie down.*

✧ I've already tried that, but it didn't | do any good.
| help.
Maybe you're right. I'll give it a try.

Repeat Practice 1 on the previous page. Continue the conversation.
Student B: Listen to your partner's problem and give him/her advice. Choose from the pictures below.
Student A: You've already tried it.

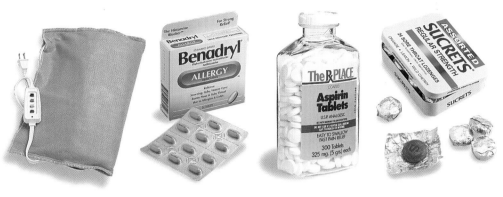

try a heating pad   take allergy pills   take aspirin   try throat lozenges

try hot milk before bed   take cold capsules   see a dentist   put on ointment

Repeat Practice 1 on the previous page. **Student B** gives advice as above. This time, **Student A** agrees to try it.

LISTEN TO THIS

Alan is telling his wife Liz about his health problems. As you listen, write down each of the problems that Alan describes. Then write down Liz's advice.

Alan's symptoms	Liz's advice
....	....
....	....
....	....
....	....

CONVERSATION 2

I'D LIKE TO GET THIS PRESCRIPTION FILLED.

Do you usually take medicine when you don't feel well?

Do you ever use home remedies or cures?

Pronunciation Focus

Listen to the linked sounds in these phrases.

help you   while I'm here

quite a bit   suggest anything

clear up   here's your

Now listen to the conversation again and mark the linked sounds. Then practice the conversation again.

Pharmacist: Can I help you?

Customer: Yes, please. I'd like to get this prescription filled.

Pharmacist: OK. It'll be a few minutes.

Customer: Oh, while I'm here..., my daughter was coughing quite a bit last night. Can you suggest anything?

Pharmacist: How old is your daughter?

Customer: She's four.

Pharmacist: This is a good children's cough syrup. Give her two teaspoons before she goes to bed. If her cough doesn't clear up in a day or two, you should take her to the doctor.

Customer: I will. Thanks.

Pharmacist: And here's your prescription.

Customer: Are there any special instructions?

Pharmacist: They're on the bottle. You have to take it on an empty stomach. That means at least one hour before meals or two hours after.

Customer: OK. And thanks again.

1. TALKING ABOUT PRESCRIPTIONS

✦ Are there any special instructions?
Is there anything special I should do?

✧ You have to │ *take it on an empty stomach.*
│ *shake it well before you use it.*
You can't *take aspirin with this medicine.*

✦ I will.
I won't.

Practice 1

Look at the drug warning labels below and decide with your partner what they mean. Then match the labels with the cues.

1. take all the medicine
2. keep it in the refrigerator
3. shake the bottle first
4. chew this medicine

5. take this with a meal
6. don't eat or drink this
7. keep it away from children
8. don't sit out in the sun

Practice 2

Now, role-play a pharmacist and a customer. Start like this, then follow the model above:

Student A: I'd like to get this prescription filled.
Student B: OK. It'll be a few minutes.
Student A: Are there any special instructions?
Student B: Yes…

Student B gives the following warnings.

1. take this with lots of water
2. can't take aspirin with this

Practice 3

Reverse roles. **Student A** gives the following warnings.

1. keep this in the refrigerator
2. can't drink alcohol with this medication

2. ASKING ABOUT NON-PRESCRIPTION DRUGS

✦ *My daughter was coughing quite a bit last night.*

Can you suggest anything?
What do you recommend for | a bad cough?
| that?

✧ This is a good | children's cough syrup.
Try (giving her) this |

Student A: You are a customer asking the pharmacist for advice. Describe your problem, using the cues given.
Student B: You are the pharmacist. Choose the best advice from the list below.

Customer	Pharmacist
1. played tennis yesterday/have stiff muscles now	• try these non-drowsy allergy pills
2. cold and flu season/am worried about getting sick	• try using this muscle ointment
3. have bad allergies/allergy pills make me sleepy	• take some good vitamin pills

Follow the instructions for Practice 1. Now, **Student B** is the customer and **Student A** is the pharmacist.

Customer	Pharmacist
1. studying a lot recently/always have dry, red eyes	• try chewing these antacid pills
2. went jogging this morning/have twisted ankle	• try wrapping it with this elastic bandage
3. ate spicy food for lunch/have terrible heartburn	• try using these eye drops

LISTEN TO THIS

🔊 You will hear a pharmacist talking to three customers. As you listen, number each picture in order. Below each picture, write down what the customer buys.

(Student A looks at this page. Student B looks at the next page.)

Some people prefer "home remedies" to other cures. Some examples are eating chicken soup to cure a cold, or putting vinegar on sunburn to stop the pain.

Practice 1

You are going to interview your partner about his/her family's home remedies for common health problems. Ask what he/she recommends for the following, and take brief notes.

The problem	Your partner's home remedy
The common cold	
Hiccups	
Insomnia	

Practice 2

Now, your partner will interview you. Talk about your family's home cures.

Practice 3

With your partner, join another pair of students. Describe your partner's home remedies. Were any of the home cures different? Are there any you might try?

(Student B looks at this page. Student A looks at the previous page.)

Some people prefer "home remedies" to other cures. Some examples are eating chicken soup to cure a cold, or putting vinegar on sunburn to stop the pain.

Practice 1

Your partner is going to interview you about your family's home remedies for common health problems and injuries.

Practice 2

Now, interview your partner. Ask what he/she recommends for the following, and take brief notes.

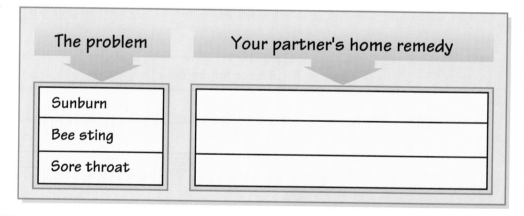

The problem	Your partner's home remedy
Sunburn	
Bee sting	
Sore throat	

Practice 3

With your partner, join another pair of students. Describe your partner's home remedies. Were any of the home cures different? Are there any you might try?

What is an attic?

What do you think people keep there?

What do you think you would find in *your* grandparents' attic?

Martin: Thanks for helping me clean out my grandmother's attic.

Ken: Glad to do it. It's interesting.

Martin: Wow! What a collector! She never threw anything out.

Ken: You're not kidding. Hey, what's this thing?

Martin: It's a coffee grinder. You use it for grinding beans to make coffee.

Ken: How do you use it?

Martin: Let's see if I can remember..., oh, yeah. First, you put the coffee beans in the top. Then you keep turning this handle until the beans are all ground up.

Ken: OK. What next?

Martin: Next, you open this little drawer at the bottom. All the ground coffee is in there.

Ken: OK. How do you make the coffee?

Martin: After that, you fill a coffeepot with cold water and put the coffee in this little basket. Then you put the basket in the pot. Put the pot on the stove and let it boil for a couple of minutes. After it boils, turn the heat down and wait another ten minutes. That's it.

Ken: Gee, Martin. That sounds good. I'd love a cup of coffee.

Martin: Sure thing. Is instant OK?

1. DESCRIBING WHAT OBJECTS ARE USED FOR

✦ What's this thing?
What's this thing used for?

◇ It's a *coffee grinder*. | You use it for *grinding coffee beans*.
| It's used to *grind coffee beans*.

Practice 1

Below are some kitchen utensils from kitchens around the world.

Student A: Ask what two objects below are and what they are used for.
Student B: Choose from the cues below to answer.
Then reverse roles.

Student A

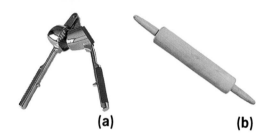

(a)   (b)

(c)   (d)

Student B

Steamer basket
for steam-cooking foods

Garlic crusher
to crush cloves of garlic

Rolling pin
for making pastry

Pasta maker
to make fresh pasta

Practice 2

Here are four other objects from around the world. With your partner, decide what they are used for. Compare your ideas with your classmates. Which of these objects do you think are still used today?

piñata/Mexico

jack-o'-lantern/North America

abacus/Asia

wooden shoes/Netherlands

2. GIVING INSTRUCTIONS

◆ How do you | use | it? | make | ◆ Show | me how to | use | it. Tell | | make | How does it work?	✧ First, you *put the coffee beans in the top.* Then you *keep turning this handle.* Next, you *open this little drawer.* After that, you *fill a coffeepot with cold water.*

Practice 1

Choose one of the objects from the previous page or another object you have used. Tell your partner how to use it. When you have finished, reverse roles. Start like this:

Student A: A.. is used ....
Student B: How do you use it?
Student A: First,…

Practice 2

Take turns asking and telling your partner how to make or do something. Choose from the lists below or use your own ideas. Your answer should include at least four steps.

- rice
- iced tea
- instant noodles
- an ice-cream sundae

- program a VCR to record a TV show
- make a collect telephone call
- send a fax
- copy a cassette tape

LISTEN TO THIS

▭ You will hear Sheila, an art teacher, explaining to her class how to make a papier-mâché bowl. Listen, and number the steps.

Paste Recipe

.... Mix it with your hands

.... Add 1½ cups of water to 1 cup of flour

.... Add about ¼ cup of carpenter's glue

.... Mix it by hand again

Bowl Directions

.... Cover the balloon with plastic food wrap

.... Tear a newspaper into strips

.... Cover the plastic wrap with paste

.... Put 15 to 20 layers on

.... Let dry thoroughly

.... Put a strip of paper on the wet paste area and smooth over with more paste

.... Pop the balloon and remove it and the plastic wrap

.... Blow up a balloon

When you and your family go on a trip or out for the day, how do you prepare?
What kinds of details do you think about?

Denise: Hey, Terumi, would you like to get away from the city and come to Lake Benjamin with me and my family next week?

Terumi: I'd love to. Do I need anything?

Denise: Well, the first thing is a sleeping bag.

Terumi: I don't get it. What do I need a sleeping bag for?

Denise: For sleeping in, of course. You can share our tent.

Terumi: Do you mean this is a camping trip?

Denise: That's right, so insect repellent is a good idea.

Terumi: Why do I need that?

Denise: Oh! You should use insect repellent there, or you'll get eaten alive!

Terumi: What else will I need?

Denise: You might need an extra set of warm clothes.

Terumi: Why do I need those? It's the middle of summer!

Denise: Just in case it rains or suddenly turns cold.

Terumi: Good thinking.

Pronunciation Focus

Listen to the final [t] sound in the following phrases.

next week	insect repellent
first thing	might need

Notice that the [t] sound blends with the consonant at the beginning of the next word.

1. DISCUSSING NEEDS AND REQUIREMENTS

✦ Do I need anything?
What (else) | will | I need?
          | do |

✧ The first thing (you need) is *a sleeping bag.* And you (might) need *an extra set of warm clothes.*	✧ No. Nothing.

Practice

You and your partner are going camping by a lake for three days. First, decide on the four most important things you'll need to take. Then, ask your partner what he/she thinks you'll need and write those items in the space provided below. Reverse roles.

Use two of these ideas plus two of your own.

Your list   **Your partner's list**

....

....

....

....

2. GETTING CLARIFICATION

✦ I don't get it. | What do I need | *a sleeping bag* | for?
                               | that |
               | Why do I need *warm clothes?*

✧ (You need | *a sleeping bag*) | for *sleeping in.*
            | one) | to *sleep in.*
You (might) need them (just) in case *it turns cold.*

Practice 1

Look at the items your partner suggested in Practice 1 above. Ask why you need them. Reverse roles.

Practice 2

Student A: You are going to have a birthday party next Saturday night. Ask your partner what he/she thinks you'll need.
Student B: Tell your partner two things.
Student A: Find out what you need them for.
Reverse roles and think of two more things.

3. TALKING ABOUT CONSEQUENCES

◆ *Insect repellent* is a good idea.
You | should | *take insect repellent.*
　　| have to |

✧ Why do I need that?

◆ You | should | *use insect repellent, or you'll* | *get eaten alive!*
　　| have to |
Use insect repellent so you *don't*

Practice 1

Student A: A friend of yours is going to France for two weeks. Decide four things he has to take. Choose three of the items from List A. Choose from List B to find the reason. Add one idea of your own.
Student B: You've never traveled before either. Ask your partner why your friend needs the selected items.
Follow this model:

A: He has to take his passport.
B: Why does he need that?
A: He has to take his passport so he *can* enter the country.
　　He has to take his passport or he *can't* enter the country.

List A	List B
• get a visitor's visa	• will/won't have a place to stay
• take guide books	• can/can't order in restaurants
• have a hotel reservation	• can/can't enter the country
• take some French francs	• will/won't get sore feet
• buy a French phrase book	• can/can't get help in an emergency
• have the address of (your country's) embassy	• will/won't have to change money at the airport
• take a pair of comfortable shoes	• will/won't be easier to make plans

Practice 2

Follow the instructions for Practice 1. This time, **Student B** talks about what the friend should take. Start like this:

B: He should take *a pair of comfortable shoes.*
　　A pair of comfortable shoes is a good idea.
A: Why?

LISTEN TO THIS

▭ Harriet is going to visit her friend Nicki in Aspen, Colorado, for a week. They are on the phone discussing what Harriet needs to bring. Listen for the following items that Nicki tells Harriet to bring, and write the reason the items are needed.

Items	Reasons
sunglasses	....
shorts	....
sunscreen	....
a nice dress	....
comfortable clothes	....

(Student A looks at this page. Student B looks at the next page.)

You are preparing for a visitor on an exchange program to visit for three weeks in September. The visitor, a 23-year-old woman, is very interested in learning about your culture.

Practice 1

Think of a traditional craft, recipe, or game from your country. Tell your partner about it. Be sure to choose something simple. Your partner will ask you what equipment is necessary, and how to make/do it.
You are telling your partner how to ....

Practice 2

Your partner is preparing a list of things that the visitor should bring for a three-week vacation in September. Ask your partner for at least five items the visitor will or might need. Be sure to get the reason.

Item	Why it's necessary
1.	1.
2.	2.
3.	3.
4.	4.
5.	5.

PERSON TO PERSON

STUDENT B

(Student B looks at this page. Student A looks at the previous page.)

You are preparing for a visitor on an exchange program to visit for three weeks in September. The visitor, a 23-year-old woman, is very interested in learning about your culture.

Practice 1

Your partner is going to give you all the information you need about a traditional craft, recipe, or game he/she knows about. Find out what you need, and then find out how to make/do it. Use the information to fill in the spaces below. Your partner is telling you how to ....

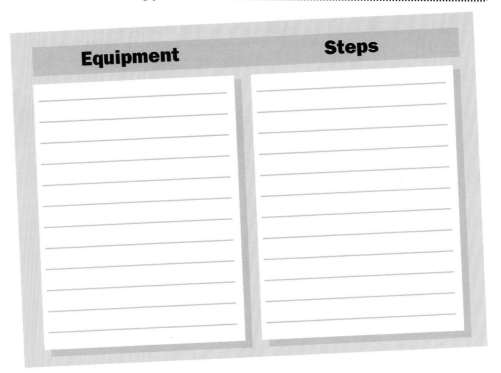

Equipment

Steps

Discuss any of the instructions that you disagree with, or don't understand.

Practice 2

Think of at least five items that the visitor will need for a 3-week September visit. Your partner will ask you about what they'll need. For each item you mention, be sure to say why the visitor will need it.

CONVERSATION 1
WHAT KIND OF PLACE IS THAT?

Where do you like to stay on vacation?

What are the two most important things to think about when you choose a hotel?

Agent:		So, how can I help you?
Mrs. Evans:		My husband and I are going to Vancouver next month. We don't usually do this, ... but we'd like to stay in a first-class hotel for a change.
Agent:		Why don't you try the York Hotel?
Mrs. Evans:		How much is it?
Agent:		A double room is $200 a night.
Mrs. Evans:		Where is it?
Agent:		It's near the center of town.
Mrs. Evans:		Does it have parking?
Agent:		Yes. Here. Take a look at their brochure.
Mrs. Evans:		This looks perfect. OK, I'd like to reserve a double room from September twenty-third to the thirtieth under the name of Mr. and Mrs. Henry Evans.

1. ASKING ABOUT TYPES OF HOTELS

✦ We'd │ like to stay in *a first-class hotel.*
I'd │
Can you recommend *a nice bed-and-breakfast?*

✧ Why don't you try *the York Hotel?*
You could try *Harbor House B & B.*

Practice 1

Student A: Your partner is a travel agent. Ask him/her about the following types of accommodations.

1. a family resort hotel

2. a large luxury hotel

Student B: Choose from the places below to make a recommendation.

Practice 2

Reverse roles. **Student B** asks **Student A** about these types of accommodations.

1. a chain motel

2. a bed-and-breakfast

2. ASKING FOR DETAILS

✦ Where is it?
✧ It's *near the center of town.*

✦ Does it have │ *parking?*
Is there │ *a swimming pool?*

✧ Yes, │ it does. there is.	✧ No, │ I'm sorry, it doesn't. I'm afraid there isn't.

Student A: Cover the answers on the chart below. Ask your partner for details about The White Sands and The Imperial Hotel.
Student B: Use the pictures on the previous page and the chart below to answer.

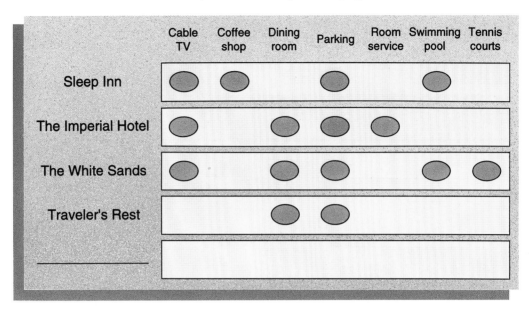

	Cable TV	Coffee shop	Dining room	Parking	Room service	Swimming pool	Tennis courts
Sleep Inn	●	●		●		●	
The Imperial Hotel	●		●	●	●		
The White Sands	●		●	●		●	●
Traveler's Rest			●	●			
_____							

Reverse roles. This time, **Student B** covers the answers on the chart and asks about the Sleep Inn and the Traveler's Rest.

Think about the most interesting or best hotel you've stayed at, and add it to the chart above. Your partner will ask you for details about it. Reverse roles.

3. MAKING A RESERVATION

◆ I'd like to reserve *a double room.*

◇ Certainly. For what dates?

◆ From *September twenty-third* to *the thirtieth.*
For *the night of August twenty-second.*

◇ And could I have your name, please?

Find a partner you haven't worked with yet. Choose one of the places you discussed and make a reservation. Reverse roles.

▭ A woman is checking into the Shamrock Motel. Listen to her conversation with the front desk clerk and answer the following questions.
1. How much are the rooms? ....
2. Put a check (✔) beside the services mentioned by the hotel clerk.

...... parking   .... vending machines

...... coffee shop   .... laundry service

...... room service   .... cable TV

What services would you expect to find in a luxury hotel?
How about in a smaller, less expensive hotel?

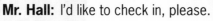

Mr. Hall: I'd like to check in, please.

Clerk: Do you have a reservation?

Mr. Hall: Yes, the name is Hall. John Hall. It's for three nights.

Clerk: Here it is. Could you fill out the registration form for me? And I'll need your credit card.

Mr. Hall: Here you are. And, do you have a room overlooking the pool?

Clerk: Yes, certainly. Do you need any help with your bags?

Mr. Hall: No, that's all right. I can manage.

Clerk: Front desk. Can I help you?

Mr. Hall: Yes. This is John Hall in Room 1436. I forgot to pack my razor. Can I get one?

Clerk: Just call Courtesy Services at extension 105.

Mr. Hall: Thank you.

Pronunciation Focus

Can is usually unstressed. The vowel is reduced to the point that there is almost no sound.

I can manage.
Can I help you?
Can I get one?

Now practice the conversation. Pay attention to unstressed *can*.

1. CHECKING IN

+ I'd like to check in, please.

✧ Do you have a reservation?

+ Yes. The name is *Hall*.
  It's for *three nights*.

Practice

Role-play checking into a hotel. One of you is the guest and the other is the desk clerk. Reverse roles.

2. MAKING REQUESTS

+ Do you have | a room | *overlooking the pool?*
  Could I have | | *far away from the elevators?*

✧ Yes, certainly. You can have room *1109*.
  I'm sorry. Those rooms are all taken.

Practice 1

Take turns checking into a hotel. Choose from the list to make your requests.

• a room far away from the ice machine
• a room with a view of the golf course
• a non-smoking room overlooking the pool
• a double room near the ice machine
• a single, non-smoking room with a park view

Your partner will use the information below to answer your requests.

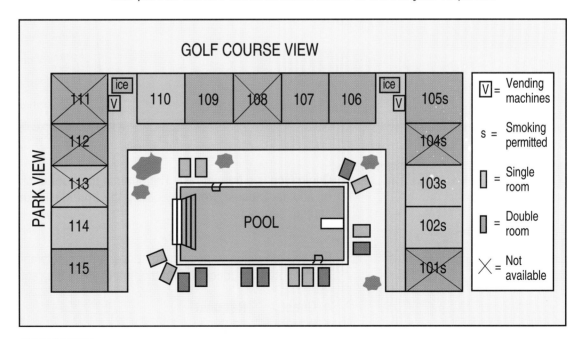

Practice 2

Student A: You have just arrived at the front desk of a hotel. Check in with the clerk and say what kind of room you want. Use your own ideas.
Student B: You are the front desk clerk.
Reverse roles and role-play the situation again.

3. CALLING HOTEL SERVICES

◇ *Front desk.* | Can | I help you?
| May |

◆ This is *Room 1436.* | *I forgot my razor.* Can I *get one somewhere?*
| I'd like to *make a dinner reservation.*

◇ Just call | *Courtesy Services* | at extension | *105.*
| *the hotel dining room* | | *120.*

Practice 1

Student A: You are a hotel guest. Call the front desk with the requests listed below.
Student B: You are the front desk clerk. Look at the directory and tell your partner where to call.
Reverse roles. This time, **Student B** calls with requests.

Student A's requests

1. You'd like to have dinner in your room.
2. You want to have your suit cleaned.
3. You need a wake-up call at 6:30 AM.
4. You want to get to the airport cheaply.

Student B's requests

1. You need some more towels.
2. You'd like to send a fax to New York.
3. You want to get tour information.
4. You'd like to arrange a tennis game.

HOTEL DIRECTORY

Service	Dial
Airport shuttle	116
Baby-sitting	107
Courtesy services	105
Dining room	120
Fax service	102
Front desk	101
Health club	110
Housekeeping	115
Laundry service	106
Room service	121
Tennis courts	111
Tour information	103
Wake-up calls	101

Practice 2

One of you is a hotel guest. The other is the front desk clerk. Together, decide on another request. Role-play calling the front desk. Reverse roles and think of another situation.

LISTEN TO THIS

▭ You are going to hear three conversations between hotel guests and staff. Briefly note the requests. Can the hotel satisfy the requests?

Guest	Request	Yes/No
1. Mr. Morales	....	....
2. Mr. Burton	....	....
3. Room 327	....	....

(Student A looks at this page. Student B looks at the next page.)

You and your partner are visiting Toronto together. When you arrived at your hotel, you found out the hotel had lost your reservations. To make matters worse, the hotel was all booked up and couldn't give you a room. The front desk clerk gave you information about two other places to stay, the Downtowner Hotel and the Ford Hotel.

Practice 1

You have information about the Downtowner. Your partner will ask you questions about it. Use the information below to answer.

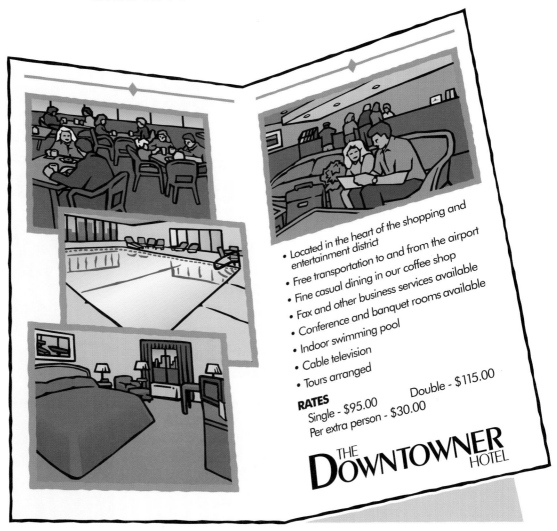

- Located in the heart of the shopping and entertainment district
- Free transportation to and from the airport
- Fine casual dining in our coffee shop
- Fax and other business services available
- Conference and banquet rooms available
- Indoor swimming pool
- Cable television
- Tours arranged

RATES
Single - $95.00   Double - $115.00
Per extra person - $30.00

THE **DOWNTOWNER** HOTEL

Practice 2

Your partner has information about the Ford Hotel. Get details about the hotel from him/her. Make brief notes.

....

....

....

Practice 3

Decide with your partner if you are in Toronto for business or pleasure. Then compare the two hotels and decide which one you want to stay at.

PERSON TO PERSON

STUDENT B

(Student B looks at this page. Student A looks at the previous page.)

You and your partner are visiting Toronto together. When you arrived at your hotel, you found out the hotel had lost your reservations. To make matters worse, the hotel was all booked up and couldn't give you a room. The front desk clerk gave you information about two other places to stay, the Downtowner Hotel and the Ford Hotel.

Practice 1

Your partner has information about the Downtowner Hotel. Get details about the hotel from him/her. Make brief notes.

....

....

....

Practice 2

You have information about the Ford Hotel. Your partner will ask you questions about it. Use the information below to answer.

The FORD Hotel

- downtown location
- close to shopping & entertainment
- TV in every room
- restaurants & coffee shops nearby
- complimentary morning coffee, tea & danish
- steps to subway
- fax services available
- show your room key for discounts at participating clubs & restaurants

Rates: *single ($55)*
double ($65)
extra person ($20)

Practice 3

Decide with your partner if you are in Toronto for business or pleasure. Then compare the two hotels and decide which one you want to stay at.

CONVERSATION 1
IF YOU LIKE SHOPPING . . .

What is an itinerary?
Do you like to travel with an itinerary or without one?
Talk about the pros and cons of both.

TRAVEL DESK

Peter: Hi. Can you help me? I'm here for a week and I need some ideas
for things to do.
Clerk: I have a few brochures here. What do you want to see here in
Los Angeles?
Peter: First, I want to see some of the famous places, like Disneyland,
Hollywood…, that sort of thing.
Clerk: Of course, and you shouldn't miss Universal Studios!
Peter: That's a good idea. What else is there to do?
Clerk: Hundreds of things! If you like shopping, you can visit Rodeo Drive.
Peter: I'm not really interested in that. What's there to do at night?
Clerk: There are clubs, concerts, plays…, you name it!
Peter: Do you know a good club? I like rock music.
Clerk: The Hard Rock Cafe is very popular.
Peter: Oh, yeah! I've heard of that place. Thanks for your help!

1. GETTING INFORMATION

✦ What do you want to | see | here in *Los Angeles*?
| do |

✧ I don't know. I need some ideas.

✦ You | should go to | the *Hollywood Wax Museum*.
| shouldn't miss | *Universal Studios!*

✧ What else is there to do?

Practice 1

Student A: You live in Los Angeles. Help your partner decide what he wants to do while visiting. Use the suggestions below.
Student B: You are a tourist visiting a friend in Los Angeles. You want to do some sightseeing. Get ideas from your partner.

(a) Grauman's Theater
See the Stars' footprints!

(b) Dodger Stadium
See a baseball game!

(c) Rodeo Drive
Shop with the Stars!

(d) Getty Museum
L.A.'s finest art!

Practice 2

Follow the instructions for Practice 1, but this time you are in New York City.

Student B: You are a tour desk clerk at a large hotel.
Student A: You are a tourist.

(a) Empire State Building
See all of New York!

(b) Yankee Stadium
Baseball, New York style!

(c) Fifth Avenue
Browse at Tiffany's!

(d) Museum of Modern Art
Contemporary art!

2. DISCUSSING POSSIBLE ACTIVITIES

✦ What is there to do?
What's there to do *at night?*

✧ If you *like* | shopping, | you can visit | *Rodeo Drive.*
go to
there's
dancing, there are *some good clubs.*

✦ That's a good idea. | ✦ I'm not really interested in that.

Practice 1

Take turns asking your partner about activities in either New York or Los Angeles. Use the cues below and the pictures on page 66 to answer. Follow the model above.

1. like movies
2. want to shop
3. want to see a baseball game
4. are interested in art

Practice 2

Think about things to do in your city and write down your ideas. Move around the room and ask two classmates. Start like this:

A: Where can you go if you like *dancing?*
B: If you like *dancing,* you can go to…

If you like...	Your idea	Classmate #1	Classmate #2
1. dancing			
2. shopping			
3. meeting people			
4.			
5.			

LISTEN TO THIS

You will hear two radio ads about places to go in Nassau, the Bahamas. What do people do at each of these places?

Ad #1 ....

Ad #2 ....

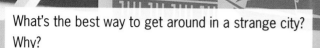

What's the best way to get around in a strange city?
Why?

Pronunciation Focus

Listen to the stressed and unstressed words in these phrases.

to gét to

from hére

in frónt of

tóurs of the cíty

a good idéa of

Now practice the conversation. Pay attention to unstressed words.

Lin: What's the best way to get to Waterfront Park from here? Can I take the subway?

Clerk: No. You can catch the number 34 bus in front of that hotel. Get off at Harbor Street. Actually, it's just a short walk from here.

Lin: Really? How far is it?

Clerk: About ten or fifteen minutes. You know, there are guided tours of the city you can take.

Lin: Oh? What does the city tour include?

Clerk: They take you by all the major points of interest. You can get a good idea of where everything is.

Lin: Hmm. How much is it?

Clerk: It's $10 per person for an hour-long tour. If you're interested, I can arrange it for you.

Lin: That sounds like a great idea.

1. ASKING ABOUT PUBLIC TRANSPORTATION

✦ Excuse me, | what's the best way to get to *the Museum of Natural History?*
| how do I get to *Waterfront Park?* Can I take | the *subway?*
| a *bus?*

✧ You can | catch | the *number 34 bus.*
| take | the *subway* to *Museum Station.*
It's | just a short walk from here.
| best to take a taxi from here.

Practice 1

Ask your partner about getting to four of the following places by public transportation. Use the cues below to ask and the information in the box to answer. Reverse roles.

TAKE CITY TRANSIT!
Cheaper, Faster, More Convenient

Bus Routes	
Sports Stadium	#67
Harper's Bay Mall	#52
Lakeshore Zoo	#17
Olde Towne	#14
The Docks	#14

Subway Stations	
The Strand Theater	Baker
Central Park	Main
Opera House	King
Mercy Hospital	College
Farmers' Market	Market

1. Harper's Bay Mall/subway?
2. Opera House?
3. Sports Stadium/bus?
4. The Strand Theater/bus?
5. Central Park?
6. Lakeshore Zoo/subway?
7. Mercy Hospital?
8. Farmer's Market/bus?

Practice 2

Write down the names of three places of interest in your city, and give them to your partner. He/she will ask you for the best way to get there. Give him/her the information, then reverse roles.
(Remember to choose a starting point.)

2. TALKING ABOUT TOURS

◆ What does the *city tour* include?
  Where does the *bus tour* go?

✧ It's a *guided bus tour of the city.*
  They take you by all the major points of interest.
  You can get a good idea of where everything is.

◆ How much is it?

✧ *It's $10 per person for an hour-long tour.*

Practice 1

Student A: Ask your partner questions to get all the details about the Walking Tour
Student B: Use the information provided below to answer.

Practice 2

Student B: Ask your partner questions to get all the details about the Harbor Tour.
Student A: Use the information provided above to answer.

Practice 3

With your partner, plan a two-hour guided tour of some part of your city.

LISTEN TO THIS

▭ You will hear a tour guide describing three places of interest. Listen and match the names to the information by drawing lines between each column.

Place	Reason to visit	Way to get there
The Grange	Has a ghost	By streetcar
Bridgeton Castle	No one lived there	On foot
University College	Bake bread there	By subway

PERSON TO PERSON

(Student A looks at this page. Student B looks at the next page.)

Randy and Emily have just arrived in Waterport for a week's vacation. They are in their hotel room discussing things that they enjoy doing.

Practice 1

Listen and check (✔) the things that Randy likes or wants to do.

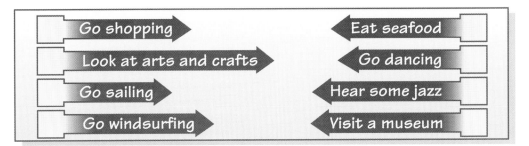

Go shopping	Eat seafood
Look at arts and crafts	Go dancing
Go sailing	Hear some jazz
Go windsurfing	Visit a museum

Practice 2

Below is a map of Waterport. You are Randy. Look at the activities you checked above, and find out from your partner, Emily, where you can do them. Add them to the legend below.

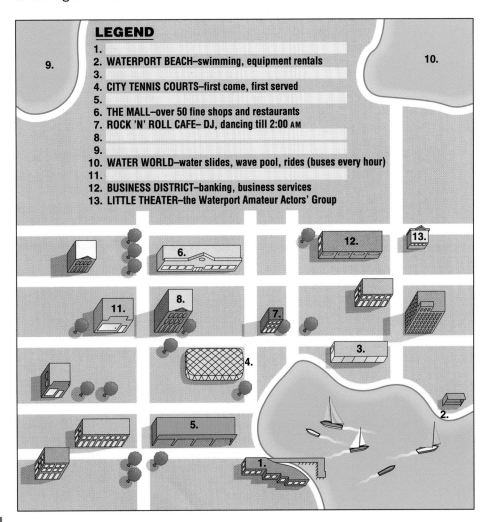

LEGEND
1.
2. WATERPORT BEACH–swimming, equipment rentals
3.
4. CITY TENNIS COURTS–first come, first served
5.
6. THE MALL–over 50 fine shops and restaurants
7. ROCK 'N' ROLL CAFE– DJ, dancing till 2:00 AM
8.
9.
10. WATER WORLD–water slides, wave pool, rides (buses every hour)
11.
12. BUSINESS DISTRICT–banking, business services
13. LITTLE THEATER–the Waterport Amateur Actors' Group

Practice 3

Look at your map again. You are Randy. Together with your partner, Emily, plan your schedule for the next three days.

(Student B looks at this page. Student A looks at the previous page.)

Randy and Emily have just arrived in Waterport for a week's vacation. They are in their hotel room discussing things that they enjoy doing.

Practice 1

Listen and check (✔) the things that Emily likes or wants to do.

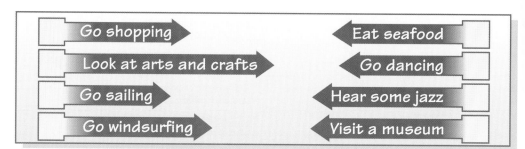

Go shopping ▶

Look at arts and crafts ▶

Go sailing ▶

Go windsurfing ▶

◀ Eat seafood

◀ Go dancing

Hear some jazz

Visit a museum

Practice 2

Below is a map of Waterport. You are Emily. Look at the activities you checked above, and find out from your partner, Randy, where you can do them. Add them to the legend below.

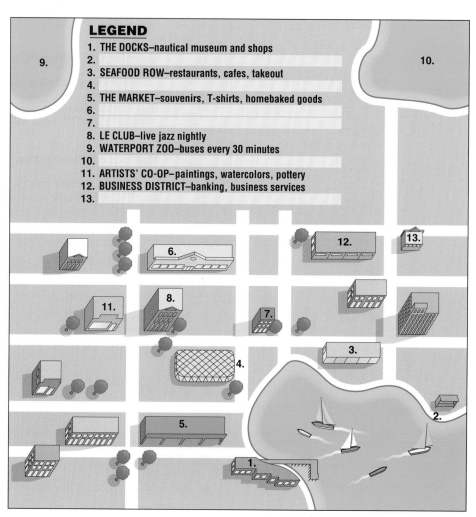

LEGEND
1. THE DOCKS—nautical museum and shops
2.
3. SEAFOOD ROW—restaurants, cafes, takeout
4.
5. THE MARKET—souvenirs, T-shirts, homebaked goods
6.
7.
8. LE CLUB—live jazz nightly
9. WATERPORT ZOO—buses every 30 minutes
10.
11. ARTISTS' CO-OP—paintings, watercolors, pottery
12. BUSINESS DISTRICT—banking, business services
13.

Practice 3

Look at your map again. You are Emily. Together with your partner, Randy, plan your schedule for the next three days.

CONVERSATION 1
DO YOU KNOW WHO THAT WOMAN IS?

What are the easiest ways to pick someone out in a crowd?
What characteristics can you use to describe someone?

Bob: Looks like a good party. I probably know about half the people.

Jane: Who's that guy?

Bob: Where?

Jane: The one next to the telephone.

Bob: I don't know. Never saw him before in my life. Why?

Jane: I think he's the guy who just moved into my apartment building.

Bob: Could be.

Jane: And do you know who that woman is?

Bob: Which one?

Jane: The one in the white sweater. I think I've met her before.

Bob: That's Linda Chang.

Jane: Is she the one whose boyfriend drives the red sports car?

Bob: Yeah, that's right.

Jane: Well, he's the one I want to talk to. He almost ran me down last week!

1. ASKING WHO SOMEONE IS

◆ Do you know who that | woman | is?
                        | guy

✧ Which one?

◆ The one | in *the white sweater*.
          | wearing *glasses*.
          | next to *the telephone*.

✧ I | have no idea.
    | never saw | her | before in my life.
    | | him
    I'm not sure.

✧ That's *Linda Chang*.
   She's the one | who *drives the
                 | sports car*.

   Isn't that *Mr. Omura*?
   He's the guy | that *owns the
                | travel agency*.

Practice 1

Follow the model above to ask and answer about the people below. Use the pictures and the information below as cues.

LUISA   ALAN   KENJI   KIM   JULIE   MARC

• works at the Mexican consulate
• is a sports reporter
• moved into the house next door

• opened the new Korean restaurant
• won the music scholarship
• teaches French at the high school

Practice 2

Get up and move around the classroom with a partner. Follow the instructions for Practice 1.

Student A: Ask about another student in the room.
Student B: Use your own ideas to answer.

2. IDENTIFYING SOMEONE

◆ Is	she Lynn	the one whose	boyfriend	drives the red sports car?
Isn't	he		wife	is a doctor?

◇ Yeah, that's right.
No. | *Her husband drives a red Ford.*
     | *His wife is a dentist.*
I'm not sure.
I don't think so.

Practice 1

Student A: You are at a party with your partner. Use the cues below and ask about four of the other guests.
Student B: Use the pictures below to verify or correct **Student A's** guesses. Reverse roles and talk about the other four.

1. Alex/wife own a music store?

2. Ana/daughter just got married?

3. Tom/son play guitar in a band?

4. Denise/mother in politics?

5. Julie/parents live in Italy?

6. Yoshi and Chie/ dog had puppies?

7. Arthur/daughter a dancer?

8. Jan/husband work for Xerox?

Practice 2

On a separate piece of paper, write a *false* and a *true* statement about a member of your family. Give the paper to various classmates and practice the following dialogue.
A: Are you the one whose ....?
B: No. I ....
    Yes. That's right.

LISTEN TO THIS

🔲 Listen as two people identify guests at a party. Match the names to the information by drawing lines between each column.

in the pink shirt	Norm	runs a dance studio
with the beard	Cliff	moving to England
in the green chair	Diane	owns racehorses

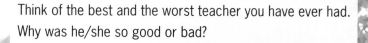

CONVERSATION 2
WHAT'S SHE LIKE?

Think of the best and the worst teacher you have ever had.
Why was he/she so good or bad?

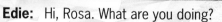

Edie: Hi, Rosa. What are you doing?

Rosa: I'm trying to pick an English literature course for this term.

Edie: Take Professor Holt's class. I had her last year.

Rosa: Really? What's she like?

Edie: Fantastic! I think she's a really good teacher.

Rosa: Why? What makes her so good?

Edie: For one thing, she's really funny.

Rosa: Yeah, but I want to learn something.

Edie: Don't get me wrong. She's funny, and if someone's funny, you pay more attention. She's also really smart, so you learn a lot.

Rosa: What do you think of Professor Vance?

Edie: He's boring. Everyone falls asleep in his class. And he's hard to talk to.

Rosa: OK. I'll try to get into Professor Holt's class.

Edie: You won't be sorry!

Pronunciation Focus

Listen to words with [r] after a vowel.

course	term
year	her
learn	smart
hard	more

Now practice the conversation. Pay attention to words with [r].

1. ASKING WHAT SOMEONE IS LIKE

✦ What's *she/he* like?
What do you think of *Professor Vance?*

✧ She's | (really) | *funny.*
He's | (a little) | *boring.*
| (pretty) | *hard to talk to.*

Practice 1

Look at the vocabulary below. Decide with your partner if the qualities listed are good or bad and write them on the spaces provided. Think of more of your own and add them to the lists. Compare your lists with your classmates.

outgoing   greedy   shy   conceited
smart   strict   considerate   moody
aggressive   open-minded   honest   hardworking

Good Qualities	Bad Qualities

Practice 2

Think of a famous entertainer or athlete and write the name below. Write down what you think he/she is like (four qualities). Then ask two classmates. Write their answers in the space provided. Form a small group and discuss your results. Start like this:

A: What do you think of ....?
B: I think he/she is ....
A: What else?

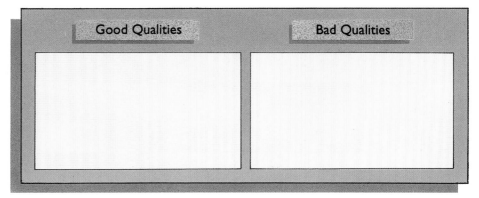

Entertainer or Athlete	
Your opinion	
Classmate 1	
Classmate 2	

2. DISCUSSING QUALITIES

◆ What makes | her | so | good?
| him | | bad?

✧ She's funny, | and if someone's funny, you pay more attention.
| so you pay more attention.
She's smart, so you can learn a lot from her.
He's boring. Everyone falls asleep in his class.

Practice 1

Think of someone you like quite well. Discuss his/her two best qualities with your partner. Choose words from the vocabulary below, or use your own ideas. Give a reason or example for each quality. Start like this:

A: My friend .... is great!
B: What makes her so great?
A: She is intelligent, so she is interesting to talk to.

attractive	gullible	friendly	sensitive
argumentative	polite	obedient	bossy
brave	stubborn	clever	cheap
generous	supportive	practical	intelligent

Practice 2

Look at the roles below. Decide on the two most important qualities each should have. Give a reason. Start like this and take turns:

A: A *doctor* should be ....
B: Why do you think so?
A: If a *doctor* is…

Doctor	Wife	Politician	Husband
....	....	....	....
....	....	....	....

Practice 3

This time discuss the two least desirable qualities each should have.

Doctor	Wife	Politician	Husband
....	....	....	....
....	....	....	....

LISTEN TO THIS

▭ You will hear two teenagers discussing a birthday gift. Write "B" beside any words that you think describe the boy's personality, and write "G" beside any words that describe the girl's personality.

.... generous   .... demanding

.... conceited   .... stubborn

.... supportive   .... greedy

.... considerate   .... sensitive

(Student A looks at this page. Student B looks at the next page.)

📼 You and your partner run the Great Dates dating service. Your job is to introduce men and women who will enjoy going out with one another. Listen as Amy talks about the kind of man she wants to meet.

Practice 1

Check (✔) the box if you hear Amy mention any of the qualities below.

I like men who...

- [ ] are sensitive.
- [ ] are funny.
- [ ] are generous.
- [ ] are intelligent.
- [ ] are open-minded.
- [ ] like to cook.
- [ ] like to dance.
- [ ] have a good job.
- [ ] like jazz.
- [ ] like to play sports.

Practice 2

Look at the boxes you checked above and tell your partner the things Amy likes. Your partner will tell you the things Amy doesn't like. Use this information to decide if you will introduce Amy to Brent or Jake.

Amy doesn't like men who…

....

....

GREAT DATES   **INTRODUCTIONS**

NAME   Brent Adams

PERSONAL INFO   33, sports reporter, has 2 dogs

I LIKE movies — especially comedies, watching sports on TV

I DISLIKE serious discussions and housework

MY HOBBIES ARE   playing golf and tennis, playing with my dogs

(Student B looks at this page. Student A looks at the previous page.)

You and your partner run the Great Dates dating service. Your job is to introduce men and women who will enjoy going out with one another. Listen as Amy talks about the kind of man she wants to meet.

Practice 1

Check (✔) the box if you hear Amy mention any of the qualities below.

I don't like men who...

- [ ] are loud.
- [ ] are stubborn.
- [ ] are moody.
- [ ] are demanding.
- [ ] are cheap.
- [ ] won't clean up.
- [ ] watch every sports show on TV.
- [ ] don't like children.
- [ ] don't respect other people.
- [ ] always look sloppy.

Practice 2

First, your partner will tell you the things Amy likes. Then look at the boxes you checked above and tell your partner the things Amy doesn't like. Use this information to decide if you will introduce Amy to Brent or Jake.

Amy likes men who…

....

....

GREAT DATES — INTRODUCTIONS

NAME JAKE BAILEY

PERSONAL INFO 34, HIGH SCHOOL TEACHER, DIVORCED

I LIKE TALKING ABOUT BOOKS AND POLITICS

I DISLIKE RUDE OR MOODY PEOPLE

MY HOBBIES ARE COOKING AND MUSIC - ALL KINDS
PLAYING TENNIS

CONVERSATION 1
HAVE YOU EVER TRIED PARACHUTING?

What's the most unusual thing you've ever done?
What's the most interesting place you've ever visited?

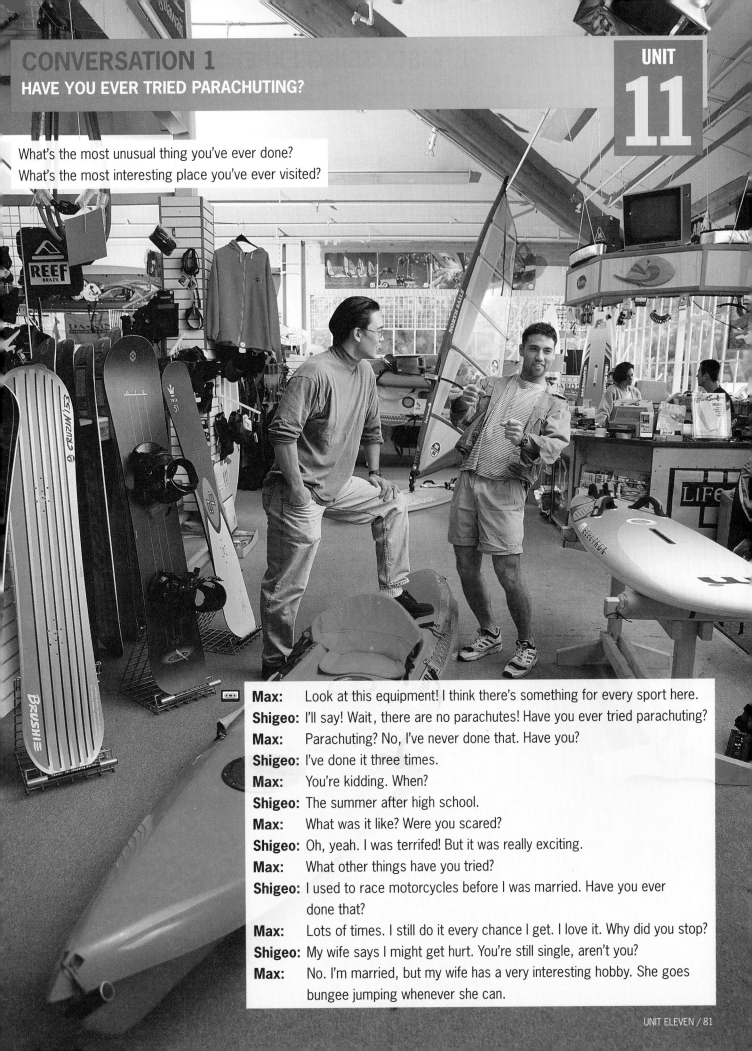

Max: Look at this equipment! I think there's something for every sport here.

Shigeo: I'll say! Wait, there are no parachutes! Have you ever tried parachuting?

Max: Parachuting? No, I've never done that. Have you?

Shigeo: I've done it three times.

Max: You're kidding. When?

Shigeo: The summer after high school.

Max: What was it like? Were you scared?

Shigeo: Oh, yeah. I was terrifed! But it was really exciting.

Max: What other things have you tried?

Shigeo: I used to race motorcycles before I was married. Have you ever done that?

Max: Lots of times. I still do it every chance I get. I love it. Why did you stop?

Shigeo: My wife says I might get hurt. You're still single, aren't you?

Max: No. I'm married, but my wife has a very interesting hobby. She goes bungee jumping whenever she can.

1. DISCUSSING EXPERIENCES (1)

◆ Have you ever | *tried* | *parachuting?*
| *gone* |
| *raced motorcycles?* |

◇ Yes. | I've done it *three times.*
| I do it *all the time.*

◇ No, I haven't.

◆ When?

◇ (I did it) *the summer after high school.*
(I do it) *every* | *chance I get.*
| *weekend.*

Practice 1

Ask your partner if he/she has done any of the following things. Put a (✔) if the answer is yes. Then reverse roles.

☐ **climbed a mountain**

☐ **tried ice-skating**

☐ **tried windsurfing**

☐ **swum in the ocean**

☐ **been abroad**

☐ **been to Disneyland**

☐ **gone snow skiing**

☐ **played badminton**

☐ **been on a motorcycle**

☐ _____

Practice 2

If your partner answered yes to any of the above, find out when he/she did them.

2. DISCUSSING EXPERIENCES (2)

◆ I used to | *race motorcycles before I was married.*
| *go to movies every weekend.*

◇ Why did you stop | *racing motorcycles?*
| *going to movies every weekend?*
Why don't you *race* anymore?

◆ *My wife says I might get hurt.*
It got too expensive.

Practice

Tell your partner about these things you used to do. He/she will ask you why you stopped. Choose a reason from the list below to answer. Then reverse roles.

You used to...

play volleyball a lot

go to Mexico every winter

have a part-time job after school

collect stamps

listen to heavy metal music

You stopped because...

you like quieter music now

you didn't have time to study

you had a knee operation

it got too expensive

you got bored with it

3. DISCUSSING EXPERIENCES (3)

✦ What was it like? | Were you *scared?*
| Did you like it?
What is it like? | Is it *fun?*
| Do you like it?

✧ I was *terrified*, but I loved it. | It was really *exciting.*
I love it. | It's really *fun.*

Practice 1

Talk with your partner about three interesting experiences you have had. Write down your partner's experiences on the lines below. Then find out how he/she felt about each one. Follow the model below.

A: What was it like? Were you *scared? nervous?*
B: I was.................................... It was ....

1... 3..

2...

How you were		How the activity was	
scared	nervous	scary	awful
excited	curious	exciting	interesting
bored	I loved it.	boring	fun/great
frustrated	I hated it.	frustrating	terrifying

Practice 2

Talk to your partner about three interesting things you still do. Write down your partner's activities on the lines below. Then find out how he/she feels about each one. Follow the model below.

A: What's it like?
B: It's ....

1... 3..

2...

LISTEN TO THIS

📟 You will hear three people talking about things they have done or still do. Listen and write down when under the correct picture. Then write whether the person says it is/was a good or bad experience.

When ....
Good or bad? ....

Think of an experience you had that you'll never forget.
Why do you think you remember it so well?

Sue: Did I ever tell you about the time I found $150?

Joe: No. What happened?

Sue: I was walking down the street, when I saw a wallet just lying there. I picked it up, and it had about $150 in it.

Joe: What happened? Did you keep the money?

Sue: No. I called the police. They came over and picked it up.

Joe: Good for you. That was really honest of you.

Sue: I had a nice surprise three months later. The police gave me the money. They didn't find the person who lost it.

Joe: Well, I'll never forget the time I lost money.

Sue: Oh, no. Was it a lot? Tell me.

Joe: I was waiting to pay for some groceries. My wallet was empty! I was sure I had about $100. I was really embarrassed! I went home and searched everywhere.

Sue: So, did you ever find it?

Joe: You won't believe it. I found it in the washing machine the next time I did laundry. I guess it was in my pants' pocket the whole time.

Pronunciation Focus

Notice how the past tense is pronounced.

[d]	[t]
happened	picked
called	searched

Now practice the conversation. Pay attention to words in the past tense.

RELATING A PERSONAL EXPERIENCE

✦ Did I ever tell | you about the time *I found $150?*
Have I ever told |

✧ No. What happened?

✦ I was walking down the street when I saw a wallet lying there.

✧ What did you do?

Practice 1

Student A: Think of an unusual experience you've had, or choose one of the ideas below. Follow the model above.
Student B: Ask questions to get more details.

Here are some ideas...

helped a hurt child

got lost in a strange place

met a famous person

Practice 2

Student B: Think of an experience you've had that you'll never forget, or choose one of the ideas below. Tell your partner about it.
Student A: Ask questions to get more details.
Start like this:

B: I'll never forget *my first day of school.*
A: Tell me about it.

the first time I drove   my first date   my vacation in ....

Find out about your partner's past experiences by asking about one of the topics below. If your partner can't think of an answer, choose another topic.
Student A: Start like this: "What was..."

Cues

• the most embarrassing moment of your life?

• the scariest thing that ever happened to you?

• the best vacation you ever took?

• the worst thing you ever did as a child?

• the bravest thing you ever did?

Student B: Answer like this: "I guess it was the time I..." or, "I can't think of anything."

LISTEN TO THIS

A woman is talking about the last time she played golf. Listen and briefly answer the questions.

1. When was her last golf game? ....

2. What kind of shoes did she wear? ....

3. How many balls did she lose? ....

4. How did everyone feel?...

5. At the last hole, why was everyone laughing?...

6. Does this woman like to golf?..

PERSON TO PERSON

STUDENT A

(Student A looks at this page. Student B looks at the next page.)

Bill and Ted have just met their friend Christine on the street. They are telling her about a camping adventure they once had.

Practice 1

Listen and take brief notes about Bill's part of the story. Do not write in complete sentences. Just a few words are enough.

....

....

....

Practice 2

Your partner has the details that Ted gave. Use the facts from Bill and Ted to put the story together. What do you think they really saw?

PERSON TO PERSON

STUDENT B

(Student B looks at this page. Student A looks at the previous page.)

Bill and Ted have just met their friend Christine on the street. They are telling her about a camping adventure they once had.

Practice 1

Listen and take brief notes about Ted's part of the story. Do not write in complete sentences. Just a few words are enough.

....

....

....

Practice 2

Your partner has the details that Bill gave. Use the facts from Bill and Ted to put the story together. What do you think they really saw?

CONVERSATION 1
WHAT DID YOU THINK OF THE MOVIE?

What kind of movies do you usually like?
How do you decide if you like a movie or not?

Curtis: What did you think of the movie?

Brenda: I thought it was great. I loved it.

Curtis: You did? I thought it was terrible.

Brenda: Why? What didn't you like about it?

Curtis: For one thing, it was too violent. There was too much fighting.

Brenda: But, Curtis, it was a martial arts movie!

Curtis: I know, but the story was silly, too.

Brenda: The stories are always silly in those movies.

Curtis: Then why do you like them?

Brenda: They're exciting. And I like the star.

Curtis: Yeah, but he can't act!

Brenda: He doesn't have to act. Those guys are in great condition. Really! It's almost like watching ballet!

Curtis: I just had a great idea! His next movie should be *Swan Lake!*

1. ASKING AND GIVING OPINIONS

✦ What	did	you think of	*the movie?*
	do		*the magazine?*
Did	you like		*the TV show?*
Do			*it?*

✧ I	thought it was	*great.*	✧ I haven't	seen	it.
	think it's	*OK.*	I've never	read	
		terrible.			

Practice

Think of three different movies that have been popular recently and write their names in the spaces provided. Write down your opinion, then ask three classmates for theirs.

Movie Title	1.	2.	3.
Your opinion			
Classmate 1			
Classmate 2			
Classmate 3			

2. AGREEING AND DISAGREEING WITH OPINIONS

✦ I thought it was *great.* I loved it.

✧ So did I.
You did? I thought it was *terrible.*

✦ I didn't like it at all.

✧ Neither did I.
You didn't? I loved it.

✦ I think it's *great.*

✧ So do I.
You do? I think it's *terrible.*

✦ I don't like it at all.

✧ Neither do I.
You don't? I love it.

Practice 1

Think of a well-known example for each of the following, and write it on the lines below. Ask your partner's opinion about each one. Agree or disagree with him/her.

Student A
1. a TV show.......................................
2. a magazine.....................................
3. an entertainer ....

Student B
1. a newspaper ....
2. a radio station ....
3. a famous book ....

Practice 2

Now, circulate around the room and ask other classmates' opinions. Agree or disagree with them.

3. GIVING REASONS

◆ What didn't | you like about it? What did | Why didn't | you like it? Why did |	◆ What don't | you like about it? What do | Why don't | you like it? Why do |
✧ It was too *violent*. It was *exciting*. *The story was silly.* I liked *the star*.	✧ It's too *violent*. It's *exciting*. *The story is silly.* I like *the star*.

Practice 1

Decide on a movie that you and your partner have both seen. Find out what your partner thought of it. Get their opinions and reasons for their opinions by talking about the ideas below. Use words below.

1. the movie itself
2. the acting

3. the story line
4. the characters

depressing	boring	gory
confusing	interesting	noisy
simple	kept my attention	slow-moving
a happy ending	scary	fast-moving
sad	childish	funny

Practice 2

Follow the instructions for Practice 1, but this time talk about a TV show that you both watch now. Talk about the ideas below. Use words above.

1. the show itself
2. the acting

3. the story lines
4. the characters

Practice 3

Talk with your partner about a magazine, a newspaper, a famous book, or your own topic.

LISTEN TO THIS

▭ You will hear two critics discussing a movie. Check (✔) the box if the speaker likes the following. Use (✗) if he/she doesn't.

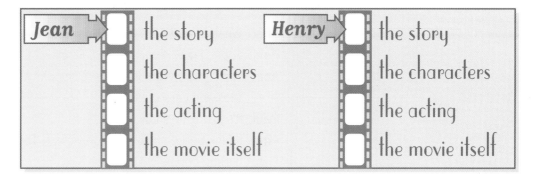

Jean — ▢ the story   Henry — ▢ the story
▢ the characters   ▢ the characters
▢ the acting   ▢ the acting
▢ the movie itself   ▢ the movie itself

CONVERSATION 2
IF YOU ASK ME . . .

Should parents decide what TV shows their children can watch?
Why or why not?
Is this an important social issue?

Ana: What on earth are those kids watching?

Paul: I don't know. *Police Squad*, I think.

Ana: Well, isn't there something funny on? All I can hear is guns and squealing tires and cars crashing!

Paul: It's just a TV show.

Ana: I think police shows are too violent. The kids will grow up thinking that hurting people is OK.

Paul: Oh, come on! I think people worry too much about TV violence. After all, you don't see our kids kicking the dog or hitting each other.

Ana: No, but I see them playing war, and they all want toy guns and weapons.

Paul: Well, personally, I think that those silly sitcoms are pretty bad, too. The kids talk back to their parents, and they're always getting into trouble! They're not realistic at all. I don't want our kids to think those TV families are normal!

Ana: I know what you mean, but don't you think that violence is worse?

Pronunciation Focus

Listen to the soft and hard [th] sounds in the following words.

soft [th]	hard [th]
earth	those
think	them
something	their

Now practice the conversation. Pay attention to the soft and hard [th] sounds.

1. SOCIAL ISSUES—AGREEING AND DISAGREEING

✦ If you ask me, I think	*police shows are too violent.*	
✧ I think so, too. I agree (completely). I'm with you.	✧ I don't know about that. I don't think so. Sorry, but I disagree.
I think *they set a bad example.*	I think *they're fun to watch.*

Practice 1

Student A: Choose a type of TV show and give your partner your opinion.
Student B: Agree or disagree with your partner's opinion and give a reason why.
Continue your discussion, giving reasons for your opinions.
Take turns being **Students A** and **B**. You can use the ideas below.

What's on TV...
police/crime shows
science programs
sports programs
sitcoms
game shows
the news
commercials
your choice

I think...
they're fine/terrible/boring/silly.
they're too violent.
they're fun to watch.
they can brainwash you.
they're a waste of time.
you can learn a lot from them.
you don't learn anything from them.
they help you forget your worries.
they are not realistic.
they help keep the children busy.
they set a bad example for children.
they can help you relax.
your ideas

Practice 2

One continuing social issue is the censorship of TV, movies, and books. Get into a group of four and talk about the following questions.

1. What is censored in your country in movies, TV shows, and books?

2. What do you think should be censored?

3. Discuss whether censorship is good or bad. Put the group's reasons in the chart below.

It's good because...	It's bad because...

2. SEEING THE OTHER SIDE

◆ I think that *those sitcoms* are bad. They're *not realistic*.

◇ I know what you mean,   but don't you think   that *violence is worse?*
  I see your point,   but I think   *violence is worse.*
  You're right,   *they're better than police*
                                                  shows.

Practice 1

Choose either Issue 1 or Issue 2 below to discuss with your partner. Together, brainstorm as many reasons as you can for both sides of the problem, and write the reasons in the chart below.

Issue #1

A: "School exams should be abolished. Grading everyday work is much more important."

B: "Exams are necessary for getting into a good university."

Issue #2

A: "High school students should be able to dress any way they like for school."

B: "School uniforms and dress codes are a good idea in high school."

Topic Issue #	
Reasons to agree with side A	Reasons to agree with side B

Practice 2

Talk about the issue you chose in Practice 1 with your partner. Use the reasons you wrote down above. Agree or disagree strongly, or if you can see your partner's side, begin your disagreement by saying: "I know what you mean, but..."

LISTEN TO THIS

🔊 You will hear two conversations. In each one, a man and a woman are discussing a social issue. Listen and write down the general topic, and whether the speakers agree or disagree strongly, or agree or disagree somewhat.

Conversation 1

General topic _____

agree strongly   agree somewhat   disagree somewhat   disagree strongly
    ⬭   ⬭   ⬭   ⬭

Conversation 2

General topic _____

agree strongly   agree somewhat   disagree somewhat   disagree strongly
    ⬭   ⬭   ⬭   ⬭

(Student A looks at this page. Student B looks at the next page.)

In many parts of the United States, people are allowed to own a handgun and to use it in certain circumstances to defend or protect themselves. Many people think owning handguns should be outlawed because guns are widely used to commit crimes, and they also cause accidental injury or death.

Practice 1

Should handguns be outlawed? With your partner, think of as many reasons as you can for both sides of the issue, and write them below.

*Handguns should
be outlawed because:*

*People should be allowed
to own handguns because:*

....

....

....

....

....

....

Practice 2

You are going to hear a panel discussion about the right to own a handgun. Listen to the discussion and check (✔) whether these two speakers are *for* the right to own a handgun or *against* it. Write down very briefly their main reasons.

	For	Against	Main reason
Roger	☐	☐	_____
Reiko	☐	☐	_____

Practice 3

Get Yu Fen's and Antonio's opinions from your partner. Give Roger's and Reiko's opinions to your partner. Follow this model to start:

A: What does *Yu Fen* think?
B: She thinks...

Practice 4

You believe that handguns should be outlawed. Use any of the points above or more ideas of your own to have a discussion with your partner.

(Student B looks at this page. Student A looks at the previous page.)

🔊 In many parts of the United States, people are allowed to own a handgun and to use it in certain circumstances to defend or protect themselves. Many people think owning handguns should be outlawed because guns are widely used to commit crimes, and they also cause accidental injury or death.

Practice 1

Should handguns be outlawed? With your partner, think of as many reasons as you can for both sides of the issue, and write them below.

Handguns should be outlawed because:	*People should be allowed to own handguns because:*
....	....
....	....
....	....

Practice 2

You are going to hear a panel discussion about the right to own a handgun. Listen to the discussion and check (✔) whether these two speakers are *for* the right to own a handgun or *against* it. Write down very briefly their main reasons.

	For	Against	Main reason
Yu Fen	☐	☐	_____
Antonio	☐	☐	_____

Practice 3

Give Yu Fen's and Antonio's opinions to your partner. Get Roger's and Reiko's opinions from your partner. Follow this model to start:

A: What does *Yu Fen* think?
B: She thinks…

Practice 4

You believe that people should be allowed to own handguns. Use any of the points above or more ideas of your own to have a discussion with your partner.

Find a partner. It should be someone you didn't work with in Unit 1.
Your friend Shelley invited you to a big party. You came alone. When the music starts, everyone except you and your partner gets up to dance. You decide to start a conversation. You may find some ideas for things to talk about in the picture below. Use your own ideas also.

Start like this: "How do you like the party?"

You and your partner are writing a *Guide to Shops and Services* booklet for a hotel in your city.

Think of five services or types of shops that a visitor might need or want. Think about quality and price and decide on the best places in town. Then note the locations of these places. (You can use an intersection, a nearby landmark, or the name of the building it's in.)

Start like this: "What's the best place to .... around here?"

Type of service	Name of place	Location
1.		
2.		
3.		
4.		
5.		

Role-play the following telephone situations. Be sure that each of you takes a turn being the caller. When your partner calls, take a message.

Situation 1:
You are calling a friend, Pedro, to invite him to go to a party with you and some other friends on Saturday night. His roommate answers the phone and tells you that Pedro won't be home until Saturday afternoon. Leave a message with all the details that you think are necessary.

Start like this: "Hi. Is Pedro there, please?"

Situation 2:
Your local TV station offers guided tours of their studios. You want to take a group of school children on the tour. When you call the station, no one is available to take your call. The receptionist offers to give the tour office all the details they'll need to arrange it. Leave a message containing all the information you think is necessary.

Start like this: "Good morning. Could I speak to someone about touring the station, please?"

You have just moved to a new neighborhood. You are new in town and don't know where anything is. Think of three things you need or want to do, and call your partner to find out where you can go.

Your partner works for "Neighborhood Welcome." His/her job is to make new people feel welcome to the area and answer all their questions. Refer to Units 1, 2, and 3 for help, if necessary.

Start like this:

B: Good morning. Neighborhood Welcome. This is .... speaking.
A: Hi. My name's ...., and I'm new in town.

When you have finished, reverse roles.

Your school newspaper wants you to write an advice column. With your partner, decide on problems that students face at school, at home, and with friends.

Start like this: "I think .... is a big problem at school."

At school

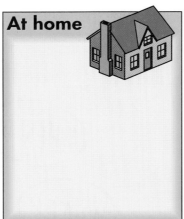

At home

With friends

Choose one of the problems you identified and discuss it with your partner. Suggest some possible solutions. When you have finished, join another pair of students and ask for their suggestions for the same problem. They will ask you for your suggestions for the problem they chose.

Start like this: "What can students do about ....?"

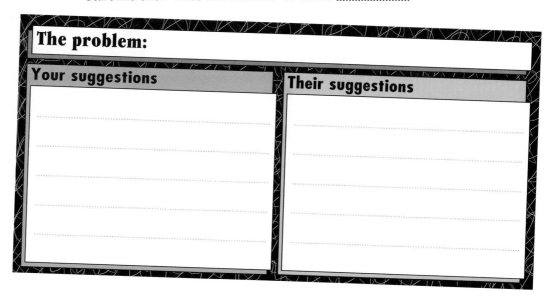

The problem:

Your suggestions	Their suggestions

You and your partner are going to take turns telling each other some good news about yourself or someone you know.

Think of something good that happened at some time in the past and tell your partner about it. Don't give too many details until your partner asks for them. Then reverse roles.

Start like this: "Did you hear about ....?"

Do you think your daily habits influence your health? Take turns giving and taking the following two-part survey with your partner.

Start Part A like this: "I have a few questions about your living habits. First,…"

PART A

1. How many hours of sleep do you get every night? _____
2. What time do you usually go to bed? _____
3. Do you take any vitamins? Which ones? _____
4. How much cola, coffee, or tea do you drink every day? _____
5. Tell me three foods that are good for your health. _____

_____
6. How often do you eat them? _____
7. Tell me three foods that are bad for your health. _____

_____
8. How often do you eat them? _____
9. What do you do to relax? _____
10. How much physical exercise do you get? _____

Start Part B like this: "Now, I'm going to ask you a few questions about your health. Please answer using *always, often, sometimes,* or *never.*"

PART B

How often do you…	Always	Often	Sometimes	Never
get headaches?	☐	☐	☐	☐
feel very tired?	☐	☐	☐	☐
catch colds?	☐	☐	☐	☐
have insomnia?	☐	☐	☐	☐
feel absolutely fantastic?	☐	☐	☐	☐

Now, look over each other's answers. Use the information from Part A and your own ideas to make suggestions about any health problems in Part B. If your partner always "feels fantastic," discuss why, using the answers to Part A.

You and your partner are talking about some people you both know. These people, with their problems, are pictured below. Choose one of them and tell your partner about him/her. Your partner will react to the news and say what that person should or shouldn't do. Take turns. Look at Units 4, 5, and 6 for helpful language. If you have time, use your own ideas and continue in the same way.

Start like this: "Have you heard about *Pete?*"

Pete

Katie and Blaine

Ed and Maria

Eva

You and your partner are starting up a community newspaper. The first thing you have to do is decide what supplies, equipment, and employees you'll need. You have a very small budget, so be careful what you choose.

With your partner, make a list of eight things you need to buy and three people you need to hire. Write down your reason(s) for needing them. Get some ideas from the picture below.

Start like this:

A: I think we should have a .... so ....

B: We also need a .... so ....

Thing	Reasons you need it
1.	
2.	
3.	
4.	
5.	
6.	
7.	
8.	

Person	Reasons you need him/her
1.	
2.	
3.	

You and your partner want to open a hotel. When the hotel is finished, you'll need a brochure to send to travel agents.

First, decide together what type of guests you want to attract. They could be foreign tourists, young families, business people, college students, and so on. Then decide on a type of hotel and the type of location it's in. Write your decisions on the lines below.

Start like this: "What kind of guests do we want?"

| **Type of guests** |
| **Type of hotel** |
| **Type of location** |

With your partner, decide on which information you want to include in the brochure to make people want to stay there. Decide also which photos to include. (Don't make it look too crowded!)

Start like this: "Which information should we include?"

You and your partner work for the Department of Tourism. Your government wants to remind its citizens that there is a lot to see and do on vacation in your country. They say that people don't need to travel abroad for an interesting holiday.

Quickly sketch a map of your country in the space below. With your partner, choose five interesting places worth visiting (regions, cities, local attractions, etc.). Then mark each place on the map.

Start like this: "What places can you think of?"

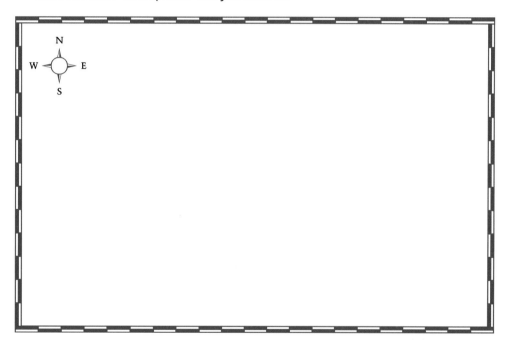

With your partner, say why you chose each of these places and write your reasons below.

Your country has just bought a small island in the South Pacific. It is three miles long and half a mile wide. One entire side of the island is sandy beach. You and your partner were chosen to design the island as a resort. The tourists might be families, couples, or college students. Think about how many and what kinds of hotels you need, and what types of activities you want to offer. Make brief notes of your ideas in the spaces provided below.

When you have made your final decisions, mark the locations on the map. Here is what the island looks like:

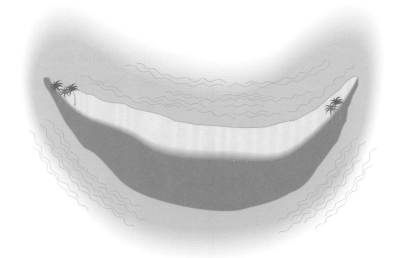

Start like this: "How many luxury hotels do we need?"

Start like this: "People like water sports, so we need..."

Start like this: "What else do we need?"

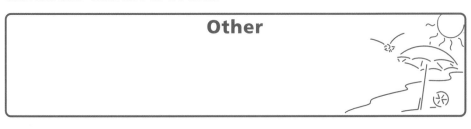

You and your partner have written a new TV soap opera. The casting director wants to know everything about the four main characters so she can hire the right actors.

Get together with your partner and create descriptions for the two men and two women who will star. Use some of the words below to help you get started; then discuss the relationships between characters.

Occupations: *banker, homemaker, bus driver, flight attendant, nurse, student, politician, secretary, writer, dancer*

Descriptions: *attractive, unattractive, handsome, beautiful, cute, kind, greedy, generous, cruel, understanding*

Start like this: "What should we name the first character?"

CASTING FORM

Character #1
Name: _____
Age: _____ Occupation: _____
Description: _____

Character #2
Name: _____
Age: _____ Occupation: _____
Description: _____

Character #3
Name: _____
Age: _____ Occupation: _____
Description: _____

Character #4
Name: _____
Age: _____ Occupation: _____
Description: _____

Relationships between characters
_____
_____
_____
_____
_____

Now, join another pair of students. Tell them about your characters and their relationships.

Start like this: "Linda is a nurse. She's 26 and very beautiful. She's also very kind and understanding, and she's the one who wants to marry Ted...."

New ideas and technology have always brought about changes in our lives and communities. How have things changed since you were very young? Since your parents were young? Or your grandparents?

Look at the topics below and talk about them with your partner. Think of as many things as you can that used to be true about them. Say when you think they changed. Finally, say whether you think the changes are good or bad. Briefly write your ideas in the space.

Start like this:

A: How has the *family* changed?

B: *It* used to ...., but now *it* ....

or

      Now, *it* ...., but *it* used to ....

	What is it like now?	**What was it like then?**	**Why?**
Family			
Transportation			
Entertainment			

The age at which young adults can legally do certain things is different from place to place. For example, in some countries you can get a driver's license at age 16; in others the legal age is 18. The government is thinking of changing some of these ages in your country. Their suggestions are in the chart below. Look at the chart and check whether you think this age is right, should be lower, or should be higher. Then get into a group of four. Take turns choosing one of the items below and asking the other group members' opinions. When you answer, be sure to give a reason for your choice. Agree or disagree with others' opinions.

Start like this: "Do you think *16* is the right age to *get a driver's license?*"

	New suggested legal age.	This is the right age.	The age should be lower.	The age should be higher.
Get a driver's license 	16			
Get a part-time job 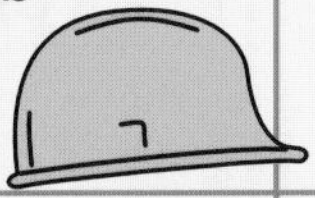	14			
Vote in elections 	21			
Get married without permission 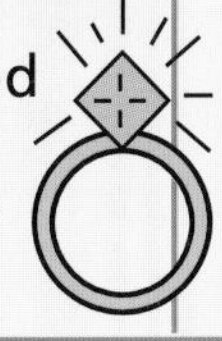	18			

Your personality is very important when you choose a profession—especially one that is risky or has a lot of responsibility. You and your partner are going to interview two people in your class to try to find out a little about their personalities. Then you are going to choose occupations for them.

First, on a separate piece of paper, write the names of two occupations. Then find a partner to work with later. Each of you interviews another classmate. Write the name in the space provided. Check (✔) *Yes* or *No* for their answers.

Start like this: "Would you ever *stay in a job you didn't like?*"

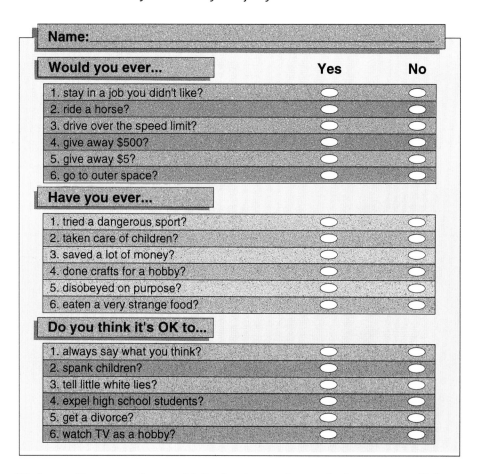

Name:	Yes	No
Would you ever...		
1. stay in a job you didn't like?	◯	◯
2. ride a horse?	◯	◯
3. drive over the speed limit?	◯	◯
4. give away $500?	◯	◯
5. give away $5?	◯	◯
6. go to outer space?	◯	◯
Have you ever...		
1. tried a dangerous sport?	◯	◯
2. taken care of children?	◯	◯
3. saved a lot of money?	◯	◯
4. done crafts for a hobby?	◯	◯
5. disobeyed on purpose?	◯	◯
6. eaten a very strange food?	◯	◯
Do you think it's OK to...		
1. always say what you think?	◯	◯
2. spank children?	◯	◯
3. tell little white lies?	◯	◯
4. expel high school students?	◯	◯
5. get a divorce?	◯	◯
6. watch TV as a hobby?	◯	◯

Sit down with your partner and talk about your classmates' responses. Make guesses about their personalities. Then assign each classmate one of the four occupations. Explain your choices.

TAPESCRIPT

LISTEN TO THIS   UNIT 1/PAGE 3

Nancy: Excuse me. Sorry I've been looking at you for the last few minutes, but don't I know you from somewhere?
Dave: No, no, I don't think so.
Nancy: Really? Are you sure? This is driving me crazy because I *never* forget a face. Wait a minute — did you grow up in Chicago?
Dave: Yes I did, as a matter of fact.
Nancy: I think maybe we went to the same high school. Did you, by any chance, go to Central High?
Dave: Yes!
Nancy: Do you remember me? I'm Nancy. Nancy Reid.
Dave: I'm Dave Mitchell. Wow! I can't believe you recognized me after all these years!

LISTEN TO THIS   UNIT 1/PAGE 6

Shawn: It looks like you had an accident.
Donna: Yeah. Right at the beginning of the skiing season, too.
Shawn: That's too bad. My name is Shawn, by the way.
Donna: Pleased to meet you. I'm Donna.
Shawn: So, how did you break your arm?
Donna: Well, I guess you could say I fell off a mountain.
Shawn: What happened?
Donna: I was in a ski-jumping competition. I landed the wrong way and fell the rest of the way down.
Shawn: How far did you fall?
Donna: I'm not sure, but it was far enough to break my arm.
Shawn: When can you ski again?
Donna: Probably in about two months. You know, I'm really mad at myself. Last year I broke my ankle in another ski-jumping competition.
Shawn: Incredible! Why do you enter these contests, anyway?
Donna: Well! For the fun of it, of course.

LISTEN TO THIS   UNIT 2/PAGE 11

Bruce: Hi, Kumiko. Hey! What's the matter?
Kumiko: It's my boyfriend's birthday tomorrow, and I have no idea what to get him.
Bruce: Why not?
Kumiko: Well, he needs a new baseball glove. I just went to The Athlete's Center, but I couldn't afford the one he really wants. Everything there is way too expensive.
Bruce: Did you try The Sports Shop?
Kumiko: I've never heard of it.
Bruce: It's a brand-new store, so they're having all sorts of opening-week specials and sales. Almost everything is 30 or 40 percent off.
Kumiko: Great. Where is it?
Bruce: On Duncan Street.

Kumiko: Where is it on Duncan?
Bruce: Do you know the Manning Building?
Kumiko: Is that the big, yellow office building beside the Metro Hotel?
Bruce: No, that's the Manulife Building. The Manning Building is the tall, glass building across from the hospital.
Kumiko: OK. I know where it is then.
Bruce: The Sports Shop is right beside that.
Kumiko: I'll go over there right after lunch. Thanks.
Bruce: Glad to help. Good luck!

LISTEN TO THIS   UNIT 2/PAGE 14

Conversation 1
Customer A: Excuse me. Does your store sell running shoes? I was in the shoe department, but I didn't see any running shoes…or salesclerks.
Clerk: I'm sorry about that. Our running shoes are in Sporting Goods.
Customer A: That makes sense. And where is that department?
Clerk: Sporting Goods is on two. The second floor.
Customer A: Thank you.

Conversation 2
Customer B: Excuse me. Where's your furniture department?
Clerk: It's on the sixth floor.
Customer B: Do they sell patio tables and chairs?
Clerk: No. All our outdoor furniture is in the Garden Shop. But that's also on six. Just be sure to turn left when you get off the escalator.
Customer B: I will. Thanks very much.

Conversation 3
Clerk: Can I help you?
Customer C: Yes, please. I bought this iron here last month, and it's not working properly. Where is your repair department?
Clerk: Take that to the appliances department, where you got it. They'll take care of it for you.
Customer C: Back to the appliances department? OK. That's on the third floor, isn't it?
Clerk: Yes, that's right.

LISTEN TO THIS   UNIT 3/PAGE 19

Conversation 1
Mrs. Williams: Hello?
Pete: Hello. Is Mr. Williams there, please?
Mrs. Williams: I'm sorry, my husband isn't home right now. Could I take a message?
Pete: My name is Pete Anderson. I'm calling about the company golf tournament. Could you ask your husband to give me a call?

Mrs. Williams: Sure. Does he have your number?
Pete: I'll give it to you just in case. It's 599-7671.
Mrs. Williams: OK. 599-7671. Pete Anderson. About the golf tournament.
Pete: That's it. Thank you.
Mrs. Williams: You're welcome. Bye now.

Conversation 2

Answering Machine: Hi. You have reached the Johnson's. We can't come to the phone now, but if you leave your name, number, and a brief message at the sound of the beep, we'll get back to you as soon as we can.
Debbie: This is a message for Mrs. Johnson. This is Debbie. I can't baby-sit on Friday night, but a friend of mine can if you want. She has lots of experience baby-sitting. Her name is Mary Ann, and her phone number is, um, 892-2971. Bye.

LISTEN TO THIS UNIT 3/PAGE 22

Conversation 1

Voice: Good Afternoon. University of Miami.
Caller: Yes. Good afternoon. I'd like to speak to the Student Housing Office, please.
Voice: Hold the line. I'll connect you. I'm sorry. All the lines are busy right now. Could you call back later?
Caller: Sure. Thank you.

Conversation 2

Voice: Good Afternoon. Medical Clinic.
Caller: Is Dr. Adams available, please?
Voice: I'm sorry. He's on vacation this week. Can another doctor help you?
Caller: No, I don't think so. When will Dr. Adams be back in the office?
Voice: He'll be back on Monday morning.
Caller: OK. I'll call back then.

Conversation 3

Voice: Computer City. How can I help you?
Caller: I'd like to speak to the repair department, please.
Voice: Is there anyone in particular you want to speak to?
Caller: No. Just the repair department. I only have one quick question.
Voice: OK. I'll put you through.
Caller: Thank you.

Conversation 4

Voice: Global Travel. Good morning.
Caller: Good morning. Is Nancy Green there, please?
Voice: Yes, she's here, but she's with a customer right now. Can I take a message and have her call you back?
Caller: All right. My name is Peggy O'Hara, and my number is 444-1416.

PERSON TO PERSON UNIT 3/PAGES 23–24

Call 1

It is now 2:10 PM.
Margo: Star-Struck Records. Can I help you?
Caller: Liz White, please.
Margo: I'm sorry. Ms. White is out of the office until 2:30. Could I take a message?
Caller: No, that's all right. I'll see her at home. It's her husband.

Call 2

It is now 2:30 PM.
Margo: Good afternoon. Star-Struck Records.
Caller: Good afternoon. Is Mr. Black in, please?
Margo: Mr. Black is in the office, but he's on a long-distance call right now.
Caller: Could I hold?
Margo: Of course.

Call 3

It is now 4:15 PM.
Margo: Good afternoon. Star-Struck Records.
Caller: Hello. Could I please speak to Ed Black?
Margo: I'm sorry, but Mr. Black has left for a party at the Sheraton Hotel. Can I take a message?
Caller: Yes. Please tell him Steffi Watson returned his call. He knows my number.
Margo: I'll give him the message in the morning.

Call 4

It is now 4:45 PM.
Margo: Star-Struck Records. Good afternoon.
Caller: Good afternoon. I'd like to speak to Sara Brown.
Margo: One moment, please. I'm sorry. Her line is busy. Can I take a message?
Caller: Sure. Please tell her that her mother called.
Margo: I will.

LISTEN TO THIS UNIT 4/PAGE 27

Good evening, ladies and gentleman, and welcome. I'm sure we have all heard the expression, "Think Green." Tonight we are going to talk about ways that we can "Act Green" in our everyday lives.

The best place to start, of course, is in the home. Every day, people all over the world are hurting the environment without even knowing it. For example, busy families buy paper napkins and plastic food wrap at the supermarket. This helps them save time on housework, but after these things have been used, what happens to them? They go in the trash. In many places, especially in North America, big cities are running out of places to throw their trash. What can we do about this?

How can we cut down on garbage? Well, we can start using cloth napkins and cloth towels instead of paper towels. When we go grocery shopping, we can choose products that are not "overpackaged." For example, last week I bought a package of cookies. The cookies were in a bag, there was a plastic tray inside the bag, and then each cookie was in its own little package on the tray in the bag! That's overpackaging! We should also take our own bags to the grocery store to carry things home in.

Cleaning products are another danger. Dangerous cleaning products enter our water supply every day. Of course, everyone wants a clean house—so what's the answer? For one thing, we could make our own cleaning solutions from baking soda, lemon, and vinegar.

Now, how about in the community? At work and school, we use one very valuable item every day. Paper. Of course, we need paper to do our work, but how much do we waste? Get your school or office to recycle paper. Learn to make notepads from the unused sides of old pieces of paper.

Perhaps, the most important thing we can do is to ask our schools to teach recycling to young children. We should teach them to be careful; we should teach them not to litter. We should also teach them by being good role models and recycling as much as we can every day! Finally, plant a tree. Better yet, plant two trees.

LISTEN TO THIS   UNIT 4/PAGE 30

Problem 1
Girl: Hi, Luisa.
Luisa: Hi.
Girl: Gee, what's the matter?
Luisa: I have a problem with my mom.
Girl: Do you want to talk about it?
Luisa: My mother said I can't go to David's birthday party on Thursday night.
Girl: How come?
Luisa: Because it's a school night and exams are next week. She wants me to stay home and study. I really want to go. I don't know what to do.
Girl: Why don't you promise to come home early?

Problem 2
Woman: ...and then we'll go for coffee. Is that OK with you, Emma? Emma? Are you listening?
Emma: What? Oh, sorry. What did you say?
Woman: What's the problem, Emma? Do you want to talk about it?
Emma: It's my daughter. She wants to move out and get her own apartment.
Woman: Does she have a job?
Emma: Yeah, she actually has quite a good job. I don't know. I just don't like the idea.
Woman: Frankly, Emma, I think you should learn to live with it.

Problem 3
Girl: That Brendan is driving me crazy!
Boy: Why? What's the matter?
Girl: He's always borrowing little things, and he never returns them.
Boy: Like what?
Girl: Oh, you know, pencils, paper, money for a coffee, bus tickets—I'm starting to feel like his mother! What would you do?
Boy: Well, I'd say, you're sorry, but you just can't keep on giving stuff to him anymore.
Girl: I guess you're right.

PERSON TO PERSON   UNIT 4/PAGES 31–32

Host: Good morning. You are listening to "The Problem Panel." We invite you to call us with your problems. I'm your host, Martin White. Our two experts this morning are Dr. Joseph Fields, a psychologist, and Dr. Joan Burke, a social worker. We have our first caller on the line. Go ahead, please.
Gloria: Hi. My name is Gloria, and I have a problem with my mother-in-law. She came to live with us three months ago. I love her, but it's very difficult. She's always criticizing me. She doesn't like my cooking, or the way I take care of the children.
Host: OK. Dr. Fields, what advice do you have for Gloria?
Dr. Fields: Well, it's a big change for everyone. Have you talked to your husband about this?
Gloria: Oh, yes. Many times. It's very difficult for him.
Dr. Fields: I think you and your husband should go to see a family counselor. It will be easier for you and your husband to talk about this problem with another person. It can help you understand each other's feelings. And your mother-in-law's.
Gloria: Thank you.
Host: Now let's hear from Dr. Burke.
Dr. Burke: Gloria, I have a couple of ideas, but first, how big is your house?
Gloria: We're lucky. It's quite big.
Dr. Burke: Well then, here's a suggestion. You could put in a little apartment for your mother-in-law. You just need a small kitchen, bathroom, and a bedroom. With a small apartment in your house, she can feel independent, but she won't be alone or lonely. Remember, it's a big change for her, too. She needs to have something to do.
Gloria: Hmm. We could, but it'll be expensive. I don't know....
Host: I'm sorry, we have a lot of callers waiting. Gloria, you've received some good advice from our experts. I hope one of their suggestions works.
Gloria: Yes, thank you. I'll talk to my husband as soon as he gets home tonight.

LISTEN TO THIS   UNIT 5/PAGE 35

Conversation 1
A: Did you hear what happened at Arthur's wedding reception?
B: No. What?
A: Well! Alice said that Stacy, that's the bride, left the party to get some fresh air. She was gone about half an hour! Naturally, everybody started to worry.
B: I don't blame them! Was she OK?
A: Listen to this! Alice told me that Stacy changed her mind about the marriage. She decided she'd made a big mistake, so she got into a taxi and went home!
B: Oh, no! That's awful! I wonder if they'll ever get back together?

Conversation 2
Woman: Mrs. Hill! What a surprise! It's been years! Tell me, how's Patty? What's she doing these days?
Mrs. Hill: She got married last month.
Woman: That's wonderful! Tell me about it.
Mrs. Hill: Do you remember Paul Richards?

Woman: Sure! Patty had a huge crush on him, then he married her best friend. She was heartbroken.

Mrs. Hill: Well, Paul's wife left him. About a year after that, he called Patty, and they started dating.

Woman: That's great!

Mrs. Hill: So they went out together for about two years, and then they finally decided to tie the knot.

Woman: Good for her! That's great!

Conversation 3

A: Did I tell you about your old friend Janet?

B: Janet Smith?

A: That's right. Anyway, Annie Howard went to Janet's wedding last weekend. She said they almost canceled the wedding.

B: You're kidding. What happened?

A: The guests had to wait for the groom for about an hour at the church. They were all about to go home.

B: You're kidding. What happened?

A: Well, he was staying at his parents' place about 30 miles away. And can you believe it? Their car broke down on the highway on the way to the wedding, and that's why he was so late.

B: Oh, no! That's terrible!

A: Yeah, but there was a happy ending, and now they say they have a great story to tell!

B: Oh, for sure! I'm really happy to hear it was all OK!

LISTEN TO THIS   UNIT 5/PAGE 38

Gwen: Hi, dear. How was work today?

John: Well, it was great, for a change.

Gwen: What happened?

John: The biology department got a big grant.

Gwen: How did they get that?

John: Hector Rojas.

Gwen: Hold on. Who is Hector Rojas?

John: He's the new professor of biology.

Gwen: When did he start there?

John: About three months ago. Anyway, he applied for this major grant, and he got it.

Gwen: That's great news. How much is the grant worth?

John: Seventy-five thousand dollars.

Gwen: Wait a minute! Did you say seventy-five *thousand*?

John: That's what I said!

Gwen: So, what will it be used for?

John: We can finally replace some old equipment. It's a real load off my mind.

Gwen: That's wonderful.

John: I feel like celebrating. Let's go out somewhere nice for dinner!

Gwen: Good idea.

PERSON TO PERSON   UNIT 5/PAGES 39–40

Jean: You'll never guess who called me today. Lucy Matthews.

Stuart: That's funny. Her husband Ken called me this morning. How's Lucy doing?

Jean: Great. She's never been happier.

Stuart: Why? What's happening with her?

Jean: She just loves their new house. She never wants to move. And their little boy started second grade. He has a lot of new friends at the school now.

Stuart: Oh, you're kidding.

Jean: You don't sound very happy for her.

Stuart: Well, Ken told me his boss offered him a promotion and a *very* big pay raise.

Jean: Really? What kind of promotion?

Stuart: To vice president of sales.

Jean: But that's good news, isn't it? Oh, and Jean hasn't told Ken yet, but she got a great job with a fantastic salary.

Stuart: Oh boy. Well, there's one little problem. If Ken wants the raise and the promotion, they have to move to California.

Jean: To California? Why?

Stuart: The new job is there. That's why he called me. He wants to know how we liked California when we lived there.

Jean: Oh, no. Poor Lucy!

Stuart: And poor Ken! They have some serious thinking to do.

Jean: When do they have to decide?

Stuart: By the first of the month. I wonder what they're going to do?

LISTEN TO THIS   UNIT 6/PAGE 43

Alan: Honey, can you come in here for a sec?

Liz: Yes?

Alan: I'm really sorry to bother you. It's just that I have a terrible backache.

Liz: Did you do anything yesterday?

Alan: Well, I played 18 holes of golf.

Liz: You probably just have stiff muscles. You should lie in a warm bath. I'll get the heating pad for you.

Alan: OK.

Alan: Sweetheart? Liz?

Liz: Yes, Allan?

Alan: Sorry to keep complaining, but I've had a headache since this morning, too.

Liz: You should take a couple of aspirin.

Alan: OK.

Liz: Alan, did you take that aspirin yet?

Alan: No. Maybe I shouldn't. My stomach really hurts.

Liz: You know what? I think we'd better go and see the doctor.

Alan: Oh, no, Liz! The doctor? Why?

Liz: You've got stiff muscles, a headache, and a stomachache. That sounds like the flu to me.

Alan: Yeah, you're probably right. OK.

LISTEN TO THIS   UNIT 6/PAGE 46

Conversation 1

Pharmacist: Good morning. What can I do for you?

Customer A: Oh, this is embarrassing….

Pharmacist: Don't worry. How can I help?

Customer A: I'm looking for something for pimples. Can you imagine? At my age, I'm getting pimples! What do you recommend these days?

Pharmacist: This cream is very good. Just put a little on each one before you go to bed at night.

Customer A: OK. I'll take it. Thanks.

Conversation 2

Customer B: Excuse me. Can you help me?
Pharmacist: Certainly.
Customer B: I wonder if you have anything for backaches.
Pharmacist: This ointment is very good.
Customer B: I've used that. It didn't really help. I've tried baths and massages, too. The thing is, I drive a taxi about ten hours a day. I think that's the problem.
Pharmacist: One of these might help.
Customer B: What is it?
Pharmacist: It's a back-support cushion. Put it behind you when you drive.
Customer B: Hmm. Well, I've tried everything else. I'll take it.

Conversation 3

Pharmacist: Is there something I can help you with, ma'am?
Customer C: Yes, please! I really need something for this sunburn.
Pharmacist: Tsk. Too much sun is dangerous, you know.
Customer C: I know, but I fell asleep at the beach.
Pharmacist: Try this sunburn lotion. It'll help the pain. It's also got a good moisturizer in it.
Customer C: Will it stop the peeling?
Pharmacist: Not completely, not with a bad sunburn like that.
Customer C: I was afraid of that.

LISTEN TO THIS   UNIT 7/PAGE 51

Hi, and welcome to the papier-mâché class. You may know, papier-mâché is quite an old art form. There are many, many ways to make it, but we're going to do something easy—something you can do at home using stuff you have around the house. OK? Let's make bowls.

The first thing you have to do is make the paste, so here's the recipe. First, put a cup of ordinary flour into a bowl and add a cup and a half of water to it; then mix it with your hands. That's right! Get dirty! This way you can be sure there are no lumps in it. Next, put in about a quarter of a cup of carpenter's glue. That'll make the paste stronger. Finally, mix it up again. And don't be afraid to use your hands.

OK, your paste is ready. Now for the bowl. First, tear a newspaper into strips. They should probably be about an inch wide. They can be as long as you want. And this might sound strange, but the next thing you do is blow up a balloon. Be sure to choose one that's about the same size as the bowl you want to make. Then cover the balloon with plastic food wrap. You can use masking tape to make sure it's secure. After that, cover the plastic wrap with paste. Now it gets really messy! Still with me? OK, next take one of the strips of newspaper and put it on that area that's all covered with wet paste. It should go all the way around the balloon. You'll probably want to put fifteen to twenty layers on. After that, let it dry thoroughly. It might take a day or two. If you touch it, and it feels cool, leave it another day. Finally, pop the balloon and remove it and the plastic wrap. And there you have it! Almost.

Next week, we'll talk about cleaning up the edges and decorating it. For now, at the back of the room you'll find newspaper, flour, glue,…

LISTEN TO THIS   UNIT 7/PAGE 54

Harriet: Hi, Nicki! So, are you ready for my visit?
Nicki: Yup! How about you? Are you ready to visit me?
Harriet: I've got my skis, ski poles, and boots for skiing. What else?
Nicki: You should have a pair of strong sunglasses, so you don't hurt your eyes. The snow gets awfully bright. Did you pack any shorts?
Harriet: Shorts? What do I need shorts for? I'm going there to snow ski.
Nicki: I know. You might want to wear them skiing on really warm, sunny days. And how could I forget? Sunscreen!
Harriet: I know…, the sun again, right?
Nicki: Right! But really, bring some so you don't get a sunburn.
Harriet: A pair of shorts sounds strange, but if you say so.
Nicki: Are you bringing a nice dress or anything?
Harriet: Do I need one?
Nicki: Bring one—but not too fancy—in case we all go out for a nice dinner one night.
Harriet: OK, what else?
Nicki: Bring lots of comfortable, warm clothes for relaxing in.
Harriet: Great idea! I'm looking forward to sitting around in front of the fire after a day of skiing.

LISTEN TO THIS   UNIT 8/PAGE 59

Woman: Are those motel lights up ahead? Yes! And the "Vacancy" sign is lit. Thank heavens!

Clerk: Hi. Can I help you?
Woman: Yes, I'd like a room for the night, please. The sign outside says you have vacancies.
Clerk: Yes—but only a couple. I guess nobody wants to drive in this storm.
Woman: I sure don't! How much are the rooms?
Clerk: They're $50 a night.
Woman: That's fine.
Clerk: I can give you Room 14. It's right beside the coffee shop. I just need you to sign the register.
Woman: There you go. I'm awfully hungry. Is the coffee shop still open?
Clerk: Yeah, it's open until nine o'clock. If you want anything after that, there are a couple of vending machines for soft drinks, chocolate bars—things like that.
Woman: Thank you. By the way, is there a television in the room?
Clerk: Yes, there is. We've got cable TV.
Woman: Oh, that's great.
Clerk: Well, here's your key. If you need anything else, more towels or anything, the office is open until midnight.
Woman: OK. Thanks again.

LISTEN TO THIS   UNIT 8/PAGE 62

Conversation 1

Mr. Morales: I'd like to check in, please.
Clerk: Certainly. Do you have a reservation?
Mr. Morales: Yes. The name is Morales. Mr. and Mrs. J. Morales.
Clerk: Here we are. For five nights. Could you fill in the registration card, please? And I'll need your credit card.
Mr. Morales: All right.

Clerk: Thank you. And here's your room key. Room 826.
Mr. Morales: Does that room have an ocean view?
Clerk: No. Rooms with an ocean view are $15 more per night. Your room overlooks…the parking lot.
Mr. Morales: Well, we'd like a room with an ocean view, please.
Clerk: I'm sorry. Those rooms are all taken.

Conversation 2

Clerk: Front desk. Can I help you?
Mr. Burton: This is Mr. Burton in 1205. Can I get a wake-up call, please?
Clerk: Of course. What time?
Mr. Burton: Five o'clock.
Clerk: That's no problem. We'll be happy to do that. Anything else?
Mr. Burton: No. That's it. Thank you.

Conversation 3

Guest: (To himself) I really overslept. Oh, boy. Eleven o'clock. I need something to eat. I'm starving.
Clerk: Front desk. Can I help you?
Guest: Yeah, hi. This is Room 327. Is your dining room still open?
Clerk: I'm sorry, sir. The dining room closes at 10:30.
Guest: Oh, no. Well, do you know where I can get some dinner?
Clerk: Just call Room Service at extension 121. You can order a light meal from them. They'll send it up to your room.
Guest: OK, thanks. I'll give them a call.

AD #1

Are you looking for the best in Bahamian food? Do you want to eat where Bahamians eat? Then try the Bahamian Kitchen. We're right downtown, located on Trinity Place, just a short block from the Straw Market. We offer Bahamian homecooking at its best—everything from peas 'n' rice to the freshest seafood on the island! So, for great food, great service, great prices, and a great atmosphere, it's the Bahamian Kitchen! Open daily 11 AM to 10 PM.

AD #2

More than a tropical paradise, we're a shopper's paradise! Do you have gifts to buy for those friends and relatives who are shivering and shoveling their way through winter? Come to Bay Street. We have everything from T-shirts to tableware, and more. Wander through our many art galleries and learn about island life from the oil paintings and watercolors of our talented local artists. Shop in our duty-free stores for fine jewelry, perfumes, crystal, and china. Browse in the Straw Market for a variety of hand-crafted straw dolls, hats, and baskets. The shops of Bay Street. Who knows? After you've taken care of all those people at home, maybe you'll find a little something for yourself!

Good morning, ladies and gentlemen, and welcome to our tour. This morning we're going to take you to some points of historical interest in the city. If you have any questions, please don't hesitate to ask.

If you look out the window on your right, you'll see The Grange. One of the oldest homes in the city, it was built for our first mayor 200 years ago, and still has most of the original furniture. Perhaps the most interesting thing is that every Saturday afternoon, you can come and watch them bake bread the way it was done 200 years ago.

On your left is University College. This university building is just 125 years old. It's interesting because many people claim they've seen a ghost walking through it late at night. After a fire destroyed one section, a skeleton was found. Police believe it is the body of a stone carver who disappeared while the college was being built. He and another man were both in love with the same woman. You can guess the rest!

We'll be stopping in a moment at Bridgeton Castle. This castle was built by Sir Henry Pellat for his young bride. He imported almost all of the building materials from England. Notice the beautiful stained glass windows. The castle also has many hidden rooms and secret passages. Unfortunately, Sir Henry's young bride became ill and died before the castle was completed. This castle is interesting because Sir Henry became so unhappy that he left the castle and returned to England. No family member ever lived there.

All of these places offer guided tours. If you want to go, they're easy to get to, and I can give you maps at the end of the tour. From your hotel, it's a short walk to The Grange—about fifteen minutes. If you want to try to see the ghost at University College, you can get there on the College streetcar. If you are interested in seeing a real English castle, it's best to go by subway.

Emily: Finally! OK, let's unpack and get out there!
Randy: Emily, slow down. We have a week! Maybe we should decide what we want to do.
Emily: Oh, Randy! You always have to be so organized. OK, well, I want to shop. I heard this town has great prices.
Randy: I swear, you were born to shop. I'd like to check out some local arts and crafts. Harry's wife brought home some pottery from here last summer. Do you remember seeing it? It was really nice.
Emily: Look at this view. You can see the bay from here. We should see if they rent boats or anything. I really want to go sailing.
Randy: We'll ask at the front desk later. I'm sure they'll know.
Emily: I'd like to try windsurfing, too.
Randy: We should make a day of the waterfront. I bet they have great seafood here. I can almost taste the lobster.
Emily: I'm sure that we can find you some lobster. And then I'd really love to go dancing.
Randy: It is a tourist town. I'm sure we can find you some rock 'n' roll. Personally, I'd really like to hear some jazz.
Emily: We can hear jazz one night and rock another!

Randy: I wonder if they have anything like a museum or something. I always like to find out about the history of a place.

Emily: We can ask the guy at the front desk about that, too. Anyway, let's just go out now and wander around a little. Maybe we can pick up some maps or brochures at the Tourist Information Center.

Randy: Good idea.

LISTEN TO THIS — UNIT 10/PAGE 75

Adam: This is a great apartment.

Tammy: I think so, too. Excuse me, but do I know you?

Adam: No. I'm Adam. I came with Carl. I don't really know anyone here. Carl's told me about most of his friends, but I can't match the names with the faces.

Tammy: Well, let's see…. OK, do you see that woman in the pink shirt?

Adam: Yeah.

Tammy: That's Diane. She's the one who's moving to England next week. The party's for her.

Adam: OK. And who's that guy?

Tammy: Which one?

Adam: The one in the green chair.

Tammy: That's Cliff. He works in a bank.

Adam: Oh! Is he the man who owns the racehorses?

Tammy: That's right. And, do you see that guy with the beard?

Adam: Uh-huh.

Tammy: That's Norm.

Adam: Is he the one who owns the restaurant?

Tammy: No. Norm runs a dance studio. Let's see, who else?

Adam: Wait. I don't want to embarrass myself. Which one is the hostess? Her name is Tammy, right?

Tammy: That's right. And I'm Tammy. Nice to meet you. Glad you like my apartment!

LISTEN TO THIS — UNIT 10/PAGE 78

Boy: I'm really mad at Mom and Dad.

Girl: Why? What did they do?

Boy: I asked them for a leather jacket for my birthday, and they just got me this stupid raincoat.

Girl: Oh, come on! It's a beautiful coat.

Boy: I don't care! I wanted leather. I tried on Bill's, and I looked great in it.

Girl: You know leather is expensive. Maybe they didn't have enough money.

Boy: I want to return it and get leather! All my friends have leather jackets.

Girl: They don't all have leather jackets.

Boy: Anyway, on your birthday Mom and Dad gave you what you asked for!

Girl: That's true, but all I asked for was a new pair of jeans!

Boy: I hate this raincoat.

Girl: All right, how much is a leather jacket?

Boy: If I return this raincoat, I only need another $50.

Girl: OK. I'll lend you the $50, but you have to pay me back.

Boy: Great. Way to go, Sis!

PERSON TO PERSON — UNIT 10/PAGES 79–80

Dating Service: OK, Amy. Just tell us what kind of person you like to date. Don't be shy!

Amy: Well, OK. I've never done this before. I feel kind of silly, but here goes. I guess I really like men who are funny. I love to laugh and be happy. That's the most important thing. But I don't like men who are really loud. I mean, I like men to laugh, but I don't want them to sound like donkeys!

Dating Service: OK. What else?

Amy: Oh, I like men who are intelligent and open-minded. Those two things go together, don't they? Good conversations are important. I love talking about books and movies and politics. I really hate men who think they're always right. You know? The stubborn ones who won't listen to new ideas? They always get into bad moods if you don't agree with them. I don't like men who are moody.

Dating Service: Now, Amy, tell me about the perfect Saturday night date.

Amy: Hmm. Well, he comes over to my place, and we cook dinner together. Then we put on some jazz music and sit down and eat and talk about important things. Of course, he offers to help with the dishes. It really bugs me when a man won't help clean up.

Dating Service: Sounds romantic. And how about the perfect Saturday afternoon date?

Amy: I guess maybe a couple of games of tennis, or… I like to golf. Maybe a game of golf.

Dating Service: So you like sports?

Amy: I like playing, but I don't like to spend all day watching sports on TV. It's a waste of time.

Dating Service: OK. Last question. Is there anything you really don't like?

Amy: Well, sure. I really don't like men, or people, who don't respect other people.

LISTEN TO THIS — UNIT 11/PAGE 83

Conversation 1

A: What a terrible waitress. No tip for her.

B: Well, *I'm* going to tip her. It's a tough job, especially at lunch time. I used to be a waitress, so I know.

A: You're kidding! When?

B: When I was in college. Some people were really rude, but I had to keep smiling. I used to come home at night with sore feet, a sore back, and a headache. I'll never do it again!

Conversation 2

A: Have you ever tried windsurfing?

B: Oh, yeah. I remember the first time I went. I was really frustrated. I kept falling. I hated it.

A: So you stopped?

B: No. I couldn't. My boyfriend loved it, so I kept practicing.

A: And now?

B: Now I can do it. In fact, I'm pretty good. I go every weekend.

Conversation 3

A: Your vacation pictures are great. They really take me back.

B: Oh, really? How?
A: I stayed in California for the summer once.
B: I didn't know that.
A: Yeah. It was just after high school.
B: It was a little scary at first, being so far away from home and all. But I made some good friends. I still write to a couple of them. By the end of the summer, I hated to come home. It was a great experience.

LISTEN TO THIS — UNIT 11/PAGE 86

Man: Have you ever played golf?
Woman: Uh…, yeah. A few times when I was a teenager. Then I played once more about five years ago.
Man: Did you like it?
Woman: Well, I'll tell you about my last golf game. You can decide if I liked it.
Man: OK. I'm listening.
Woman: These two guys, Max and Nick, invited me and my sister to spend a day at their country club. When we got there, the guys decided we should play golf. Of course, my sister and I didn't have golf shoes.
Man: So, what did you do?
Woman: We had to golf in our sandals.
Man: In your sandals? How was the game?
Woman: The first four holes were OK, but after that, it was terrible.
Man: Why? What happened?
Woman: We were starting to play the fifth hole when it started raining.
Man: Did you stop then?
Woman: No, because it was just raining lightly. But my sandals got really wet and slippery, so every time I tried to swing my golf club, I almost fell over.
Man: Did you finish the game?
Woman: Oh, yeah. We finished the game, but I lost four of Max's golf balls and two of Nick's. We were all getting frustrated and mad.
Man: Were you still speaking to each other after the game?
Woman: Well, wait. I didn't tell you the worst part. We were teeing off at the last hole. I tried to hit the ball as hard as I could. I slipped in my wet sandals and fell. Then everyone started laughing. I was really mad… and embarrassed!
Man: So, what did you do?
Woman: I promised myself never to go golfing again!

PERSON TO PERSON — UNIT 11/PAGES 87–88

Ted: Hi, Christine. What's up?
Christine: Hi, Ted. Hi, Bill. I just bought a new camping tent. I can't wait to use it.
Bill: Hey, Ted, do you remember the time we went camping?
Ted: I'll say! I'll never forget it.
Christine: Why? What happened, Ted?
Ted: We saw a UFO.
Bill: Wait, Ted. *You* thought we saw a UFO.
Ted: That's right.
Christine: When was this?
Bill: About three years ago.
Ted: Yeah. In July. We were camping beside a lake.
Bill: It was a really hot night, so we decided to sleep outside.
Ted: We put our sleeping bags on the beach.

Bill: I remember that the sky was full of stars.
Ted: Anyway, all of a sudden, Bill asks, "What's that?"
Bill: Yeah! I saw a bright light going across the sky. It was moving really slowly.
Ted: We knew it wasn't an airplane. It was going way too slow.
Bill: I thought maybe it was a weather satellite or a spy satellite.
Ted: A spy satellite? No way! It was a UFO, for sure!
Bill: So I told Ted that maybe the aliens might come and kidnap us.
Christine: Oh, come on! You've seen too many movies! So then what did you do?
Bill: Then *you* got scared! So we went back to the tent.
Ted: I took all our cans of food with me.
Christine: Why? Were you going to make dinner for the aliens?
Ted: No! I was going to throw everything at them.
Christine: I can't believe this!
Bill: Anyway, Ted stayed awake all night.
Ted: Then we went home early the next morning.
Christine: I guess you didn't see any aliens!
Bill: No! I made a few calls the next day. Nobody had reported any UFOs that night.
Ted: Yeah, well, they also said there were no TV or weather satellites in the area either.
Christine: So, spies or aliens! It could only happen to you guys!

LISTEN TO THIS — UNIT 12/PAGE 91

Narrator: Welcome to another edition of *The Critical Eye*. Tonight, Jean Lovett and Henry Pandit will give you their opinions on three movies that will be opening soon in theaters across America.
Henry: Good evening, America, and good evening, Jean.
Jean: Evening, Henry. The first movie we're going to talk about tonight is *The Final Chapter*. Of course, I don't want to reveal too much, but it involves politics, murder, and a writer who uncovers some deadly secrets. This movie has everything—mystery, suspense, romance, and action. The problem is, the movie just doesn't work.
Henry: Why didn't you like it? I thought it was a great story. It kept my attention. There were a lot of details to remember, but it never got confusing. I thought the story was excellent.
Jean: You did? I didn't. I thought there were too many details. I found it really slow-moving and frustrating. I mean, they didn't need the romance between the detective and the writer.
Henry: That's true, but I think they wanted the characters to have more personality. I liked the characters more because of the romance.
Jean: Well, I didn't like them. But, I thought the acting was good. I really liked Sam Foster's acting.
Henry: You did? I didn't. He was just OK. It's too bad—two good characters almost ruined by two bad acting jobs. I really thought newcomer Cassie Lane, as the writer, was a bore!
Jean: Well, I have to say, don't waste your money on this movie! The story is confusing and the characters are silly. Good acting couldn't save it!
Henry: And I say, the acting isn't that great, but the story and the characters are good enough to keep you entertained.
Jean: Now it's up to you, America! You've heard our opinions.
Henry: Now the final decision is yours!

Conversation 1

A: I see in the paper they're sending more equipment to space.

B: Oh, great. How much is that going to cost?

A: Oh, a couple of million, I guess. Why?

B: Well, I think it's a big waste of money! There are poor countries and people starving on this planet! I think these space flights are stupid!

A: I don't think so. Because of them we have TV and weather satellites; besides, we might have to live there someday.

B: Not me! I'm staying right here!

Conversation 2

A: Did you hear the good news? Our company is going to put in a day-care center.

B: What for?

A: There are a lot of working mothers there. It'll be a lot easier for them to work now. I think day-care at work is a great idea!

B: Humph! A mother's place is in the home. It's better for the children and the family if the mother doesn't work.

A: Well, I know what you mean, and I see your point, but in today's economy, many mothers have to get a job.

B: That's true. I guess I didn't think of that.

Moderator: The question of handguns always raises a lot of discussion in this country. Tonight we'll hear opinions from people from different countries. Our guests tonight are Roger from Canada, Reiko from Japan, Yu Fen from Hong Kong, and Antonio from Italy. Roger, let's start with you.

Roger: In my opinion, the laws on handguns should be changed. Do you know more than 40,000 people a year are killed with handguns? It's crazy! Guns should be outlawed immediately!

Moderator: Yu Fen, you look like you want to say something. What's your opinion?

Yu Fen: Well, I don't really like guns, but we have to ask who is doing the killing? I think most of the killers are crazy, or criminals, or crazy criminals! I hate to say it, but I think people should be allowed to own guns. Ordinary people have to be able to protect themselves and their families.

Moderator: People in Japan can't have guns at home. What do you think about all this, Reiko?

Reiko: I also hate to say it, but I agree with Yu Fen. A violent person might use anything as a weapon. Roger said around 40,000 people get killed with guns each year. I think more than a million people have a gun at home. All gun owners are not crazy killers. In my opinion, people should be allowed to own guns.

Moderator: That's a very good point, Reiko. It's like traffic accidents. Many people get killed in car accidents, but we don't talk about the millions and millions of people who drive their cars every day and never have an accident. Antonio? What's your opinion? Do you agree with Reiko or not?

Antonio: I see her point. Yes, it's true that millions of people have guns at home, and they never go out and murder people. But, her good point has another side. I've heard that there are close to 20,000 accidents in the home every year that happen because of guns. Children watch TV and see people shooting other people, but they are too young to understand what happens in real life. So, I think they are very dangerous. I think the law should be changed, and no one except the police should be able to carry guns.

Moderator: Thank you, guests. You've heard some opinions from around the world. Now we want to hear your opinion. Call, fax, or write to this TV program. We'll tell you how to get in touch with us in just a moment.